PRACTICAL

ASTROLOGY

A Simple Method of Casting Horoscopes

The Language of the Stars

EASILY COMPREHENDED

BY

Comte C. de Saint-Germain

Author of "The Study of Palmistry" (for Professional Purposes),
"Practical Hypnotism," "Practical Palmistry," etc.

Unfolding the wonderful wisdom of the Chaldean, Egyptian,
Greek and Arabian astrologers, without any of the complicated, discouraging operations required by other methods

Newcastle Publishing Company, Inc.
Hollywood, California

1/12

A NEWCASTLE BOOK
FIRST PRINTING: MARCH 1973
PRINTED IN THE UNITED STATES OF AMERICA

PREFACE

Astrology is the ancient art or science of divining the fate and future of human beings from indications given by the positions of the sun, moon, planets, and stars.

The study of astrology and the belief in it, as part of astronomy, is found in a developed form among the ancient Babylonians. Directly or indirectly, through the Babylonians, it spread to other nations. It came to Greece about the middle of the fourth century B. C., and reached Rome before the opening of the Christian Era. In India and China, astronomy and astrology are largely reflections of Greek theories ¡and speculations. Astrology was actively cultivated in the region of the Nile during the Hellenistic and Roman periods. Astrology was further developed by the Arabs from the seventh to the thirteenth century, and in the Europe of the fourteenth and fifteenth centuries, astrologers were dominating influences at Court.

Starting with the indisputable fact that man's life and happiness are largely dependent upon phenomena in the heavens, that the fertility of the soil is dependent upon the sun shining in the heavens as well as upon the rains that come from the heavens and that, on the other hand, the mischief and damage done by storms and inundations are to be traced likewise to the heavens—small wonder is it that a perfect theory has been developed, a theory of a complete accord between phenomena observed in the heavens and occurrences on earth.

Such a theory is here developed, and made applicable to the individual. Indeed the latter half of the book is so simply and clearly written that the reader may cast his own horoscope. This book renders a further service by giving the reader a greater knowledge of the twelve types of people, their qualities and their faults. By knowing these characteristics, one can be more tolerant with his fellow-men—appreciate their virtues and have patience with their weaknesses.

Personally practiced, astrology assists one to reach his goal.

PUBLISHER

June 1, 1931,
Chicago, Illinois.

Table of Contents

List of Illustrations

PRACTICAL ASTROLOGY

CHAPTER I

WHAT IS ASTROLOGY?

Among all the sciences and arts which
claim, justly or not, to reveal man or
woman's nature and to open the mysterious
book of the future, there is none more justi-
fied in its pretensions than the oldest of all
the sciences, the science of ASTROLOGY.

Its antiquity and the high standing of the
men who have believed implicitly in its
revelations, force even the most skeptical to
grant it a certain amount of the respect
which they begrudge to Palmistry, Car-
tomancy (the reading of the future in cards),
or Phrenology. Although it might seem to
the unbeliever as if the great progress of
modern Astronomy had removed from their
proud position the astronomers of ancient
Assyria, Egypt and Greece, it so happens
that the more recent discoveries among the
ruined tombs of the early Egyptian kings—
built some 4,800 years before Christ—have

9

furnished us with the most positive proofs that the great astrologers of those days were almost as deeply conversant with the principles of our solar system as the astronomers of the present century, allowance being made, of course, for the fact that they had no telescopes to assist them in their researches in the firmament.

Now, the Chaldean, Egyptian and Greek ASTRONOMERS were, also, ASTROLOGERS, that is to say, while understanding, in the main, the positions of the stars and planets as correctly as we do since the rediscoveries of Kepler, Copernicus and Newton—they also believed that these heavenly bodies exert over every human being a powerful influence for good or evil, from the day of birth to the hour of death, an influence, which, of course, personal conduct will strengthen or decrease.

In our time of skepticism and agnosticism it is not strange that the claims of ASTROLOGY are laughed at, but it is certainly a study that has lost none of the powerful fascination which it has exerted over the greatest men throughout the 7,000 or 8,000 years of which we know anything, and the vast number of well-authenticated fulfillments of prophecies by astrologers will surely go far to prove that Astrology is entitled to the name of a SCIENCE.

From among the thousands of cases of successful predictions by astrologers we mention here two which are as remarkable as they are true.

The first instance we cite from Bacon's *Essay of Prophecies:*—"When I was in France, I heard from one Dr. Pena, that the queen-mother, who was given to curious arts, caused the king, her husband's, nativity to be calculated, under a false name; and the astrologer gave a judgment, that he should be killed in a duel; at which the queen laughed, thinking her husband to be above challenges and duels; but he was slain upon a course at tilt, the splinters of the lance of Montgomery piercing his neck."

The second is a most singular prophecy by one of the most brilliant astronomers of the sixteenth century, Tycho Brahe, who improved the art of astronomical observation. In 1577 there was a comet visible, from the observation of which Brahe deduced a clear proof that the sky was not a solid vault, and from the appearance and course of which he predicted, that in the North, in Finland, there should be born a prince who should lay waste Germany and vanish in 1632

Gustavus Adolphus, king of Sweden, was born in Finland, overran Germany and when he was killed, in 1632, in the battle of Luetzen, his dead body was never found.

Whoever has read Milton's *Paradise Lost*, will remember his innumerable references to planetary influences; Wallenstein, the great captain and adversary of Gustavus Adolphus, undertook no important work without first consulting Seni, his astrologer, and it is well known that Napoleon I. firmly believed in his star.

CHAPTER II

THE PLANETS AND THE ZODIAC

The heavenly bodies that are of influence over the destinies of human beings, and consequently over all human affairs, will be given in this volume, together with their relations to each other and their various combinations, which, as astronomy teaches us, have re-occurred in regular intervals from time immemorial. We shall find the influence of each star, of each constellation, and of each combination, based on the experience of thousands of years; we shall find elaborate tables, worked out with infinite patience by the old astrologers, and exceedingly helpful to the student. The directions for using them are simple and plain and can be understood and followed by a child, as are, also, those for the use of the "arcanes," a marvelous inheritance from the ancient wizards in the shape of seventy-eight mysterious "tarots," which were probably originally devised by the old masters as aids in teaching their art, and which are an interesting study by themselves.

Astronomy teaches us that there are two classes of heavenly bodies: "Fixed Stars" and "Planets." The first are as many Suns at enormous distances from the Earth; our own particular Sun being, not the largest, but the nearest. The other class of stars are called "Planets" on account of their roaming habits, which are not, however, in any way erratic, since they follow regular routes over stated tracks, called their "Orbits." The Earth is a planet and takes 365 days and a fraction to cover its orbit around the Sun, its central ruler. The other large planets known to us are, in the order of their nearness to the Sun, our common center:

1. Mercury.   3. The Moon.   5. Jupiter.
2. Venus.   4. Mars.   6. Saturn.

(The Moon, which revolves around the Earth and with the Earth around the Sun, and on account of its nearness, has a strong influence.)

If we now add that a large number of Fixed Stars, visible with the naked eye, have been grouped, from time immemorial, into Twelve Combinations called the "Constellations of the Zodiac," we shall have an exact idea of the various celestial elements that furnish the necessary data for complete and accurate Astrological readings, or "Horoscopes,"—this being one of the first terms you must become familiar with.

So far we have not used any words or statements that are not used in every primer on Astronomy and the definition of the Zodiac which follows, is also accepted by modern science, although dating back to the very dawn of human history.

The "Zodiac" is the imaginary route which the Sun travels around the Earth during a period of one year. We write "imaginary" because it is recognized nowadays that it is the Earth that is traveling around the Sun, and not the Sun around the Earth. But this manner of expressing the idea, being in constant use, had better be adhered to for the present.

Now, as the Sun travels around the Earth, it seems to be entering every thirty days among a new set of stars, or "Constellation" which, ever since man began to take delight in contemplating the skies, have been known to be the successive monthly dwellings of the Sun, called the "Signs of the Zodiac."

Before proceeding further it is therefore proper for us to give you the accepted names of the "Signs of the Zodiac," and the exact periods during which these Constellations exert their influence over the Earth and the inhabitants of it.

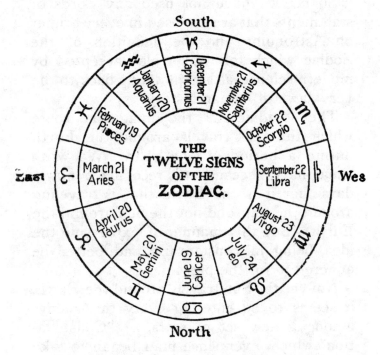

The astrological year begins with the spring equinox, on March 21st; thus:

The first Sign of the Zodiac—ARIES (the Ram)—reigns from March 21st to April 19th.

The second sign—TAURUS (the Bull)—reigns from April 20th to May 19th.

The third sign—GEMINI (the Twins)—reigns from May 20th to June 18th.

The fourth sign—CANCER (the Crab)—reigns from June 19th to July 23d.

The fifth sign—LEO (the Lion)—reigns from July 24th to August 22d.

The sixth sign—VIRGO (the Virgin)—reigns from August 23d to September 21st.

The seventh sign—LIBRA (the Balance)—reigns from September 22d to October 21st.

The eighth sign—SCORPIO (the Scorpion)—reigns from October 22d to November 20th.

The ninth sign—SAGITTARIUS (the Archer)—reigns from November 21st to December 20th.

The tenth sign—CAPRICORN (the Sea-Goat)—reigns from December 21st to January 19th.

The eleventh sign—AQUARIUS (the Water-Bearer)—reigns from January 20th to February 18th.

The twelfth sign—PISCES (the Fishes)—reigns from February 19th to March 20th.

The divisions of these twelve periods are called "Degrees" and not "Days." As the student has doubtless already noticed, there are 30 degrees (days) in each sign, except in "Cancer," where there are 35 degrees (days) to complete the regular cycle of 365 days composing the solar year; these five extra "degrees" or days are called "Epagomenes."

We cannot, in this short work, give the reasons for these various arrangements, all very logical when fully understood; it would take too much time and space and only confuse the student who, at present, is solely looking for simple rules that he may apply himself, successfully. This second chapter, with the illustration that accompanies it, has indicated to him the first Astrological elements with which he must make himself absolutely familiar if he wants to proceed smoothly in his study of this strange and most curious science.

The symbol, or written mark, by which each sign of the Zodiac is invariably indicated in astrological illustrations and horoscopes, is given in our illustration next to the name of the sign it corresponds to and again, in the next chapter, at the head of each of the twelve divisions devoted to the Signs of the Zodiac and the Types that proceed from them.

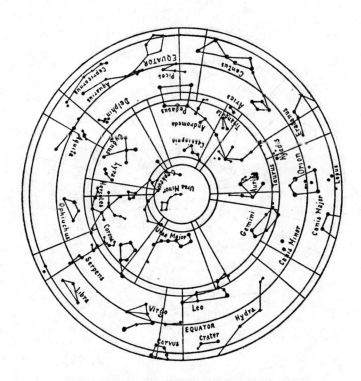

THE PRINCIPAL CONSTELLATIONS OF
THE NORTHERN SKY.

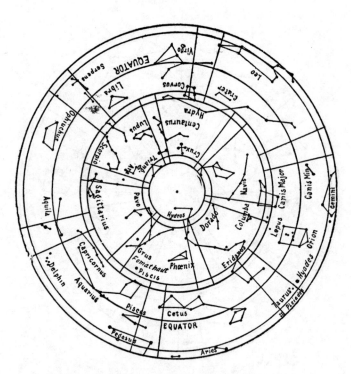

**THE PRINCIPAL CONSTELLATIONS OF
THE SOUTHERN SKY.**

CHAPTER III

THE SIGNS OF THE ZODIAC

As explained to you in the preceding chapter, the "Zodiac" is the zone of the heavens whereon are to be found the various omens or predictions which are to constitute a primary "Horoscope."

The great importance ascribed to the Zodiac by all the astronomers of the most ancient times, is proved by the elaborate and artistic representations of it, which are still to be found in Eastern countries, such as China, India and Egypt. Some of the famous representations of the Zodiac have been hewn in stone.

The twelve equal divisions of the Zodiac are called "Signs"; each of them is itself divided into thirty "Degrees" or days, and every one was born in one of these degrees. The first thing to know, therefore, is the ancient meaning of each of the signs and the type peculiar to the human beings born under it. I shall give in this chapter a summary of the leading features belonging to the Signs. Before doing so, however, I will state that the Signs have been classed into four groups, or "Trinocracies," according to their dominant characteristics.

Aries, Leo, Sagittarius, are "Fiery Signs."

Taurus, Virgo, Capricornus, are "Earthy Signs."

Gemini, Libra, Aquarius, are "Airy Signs."

Pisces, Cancer, Scorpio, are "Watery Signs."

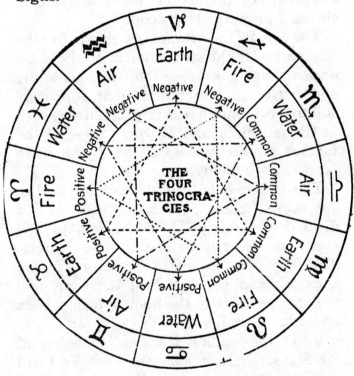

THE FOUR TRINOCRACIES.

The illustration on this page indicates

this division by means of triangles. Later
I shall have occasion to more fully explain
the importance of this classification. I
begin now the enumeration of the peculi-
arities and omens special to each of the
signs. It is the basis of all further study
and must, therefore, be given most serious
attention.

1 ARIES. (The Ram.) ♈

The Constella-
tion "Aries"—the
first Sign of the
Zodiac—exerts its
influence from
March 21 to April
19, the period co-
inciding with the
first month of the Roman Year. It endows those born during this period with
simple, unaffected manners, with an obedi-
ent disposition and yet with a capacity for
commanding (a duality of qualities frequently met with); with plenty of enterprising audacity; with a lofty, charitable soul;
with a generous heart, that will meet with
few grateful returns; with a firm will, a
superior mind, quick, brilliant, courageous,

but not lacking in prudence; with religious tendencies; often with artistic talents, with plenty of clever ingenuity; a natural gift for business; a rather combative spirit, tempered, however, by eclecticism (the power of learning from others). The will, although steadfast, may vary in its object, in its plans.

He will have a taste for outdoor sports, especially hunting.

He will aspire to the highest honors, and will not be daunted by the difficulties in his way. Should he choose a military career, he would make a success of it and gain rapid promotion.

This sign endows one with aptitudes more varied than profound; it renders eloquent. The love affairs of one born under this sign will be sudden, full of fancies and of short duration.

The subjects of Aries will get easily into passions of rage, but the fire will burn itself quickly out and leave behind no rancor or grudge. They will forget, in an instant, the injury done to them.

The opinions of the subject, be they of a religious or political character, will be very strong and ardent for a time, but that time will be short.

He will pass through many changes in his

financial status; he will own much real estate, especially country property that will come to him through marriage. He will have to stand many difficulties and law-suits in reference to these estates; women's preferences and an inheritance will bring him most of what he will ever own; but he will be lucky in his business partnerships.

He will probably be an only child, or become such by the death of brothers and sisters.

In childhood, there will be troubles or disasters in the family of the subject that may upset his career.

If the birth takes place between midnight and noon, the subject will lose his father early in life.

Much traveling will be rendered necessary by family matters or to escape enmities. The subject will make balloon ascensions, or at least climb mountains.

At the ages of 7, 19, 30, 44, the subject's family will meet with trouble or he himself will run dangers due to his own relatives.

By his own fault, the subject will shorten the duration of his life; he will have to struggle against many unforeseen and dreadful incidents that will place him in great peril.

Aries announces many conjugal disagreements and often broken partnerships.

There will be very few children, if any.

The subject will rise, after many obstacles, to high positions of trust and honor, but will not keep them, as he will be the victim of the bitterest envy.

The subject will marry too young; there will be danger of inconstancy in the marriage relations.

The professions that will probably be chosen, by the persons born under this sign, are the army, the bar and mining engineering.

Should the birth take place between the hours of noon and midnight, the friends of the subject will greatly exert themselves pushing him to the front, and he will reach high positions; if he is in the Church, a bishopric may come to him.

He will have many and devoted friends with a dangerous traitor among them, Many, also, will be his enemies, all envious of his success, but these enmities will not last long.

The physical temperament of the subject will be nervous-sanguine, if he is born in a southern climate, and bilious-sanguine if he is born in a northern latitude. (See page 75.)

2. TAURUS. (The Bull.) ♉

The Constellation "Taurus"—the second sign of the Zodiac—exerts its influence from April 20 to May 19.

It endows the persons born during this period with a stubborn disposition; it makes them rebellious to advice, exaggerately proud, difficult of approach, and fond of opposition to the point of starting a controversy, or a fight for the sole purpose of coming out victorious. Slow to get excited and slow to calm down, the subjects of Taurus will harbor a grudge for a long time and will be hard to reconcile.

Of course, all these idiosyncrasies may be modified, even overcome by surroundings, education, etc. We are only enumerating here inborn tendencies or instincts that can always be fought against and triumphed over.

This sign gives the subject a mind straightforward, just, inquisitive and shrewd; it makes him hard to fathom and endows him with the essential qualities of a diplomat.

The impressions, when received, are violent but changeable; the passions fiery, but not persistent.

The subjects whom this sign influences are generally very much attached to their sentiments and their opinions; they are taciturn and tenacious; their will is steady, persevering and determined to reach its end at almost any cost.

They are fit to command, to govern; there is a great probability that their brain power will prove of so superior a kind that they will be carried up to celebrity almost unwittingly.

Sometimes the sign of Tarus gives the subject a taste for agriculture; it is certainly conducive to a liking for choice food, while it renders the subject patient in all his undertakings and fond of a well-earned repose of mind and body.

The subjects of Taurus are essentially conservative in their ideas, their actions, and even their ambition toward high offices.

In love matters, they are (with many exceptions) of a fickle, yet jealous, disposition.

This sign always brings about severe struggles, also illnesses caused either by excess of work or by a too great indulgence in good living.

There will be a gathering of an important amount of personal property; but it will be in some danger of being frittered away, either by lawsuits, or by loss of employment, or through intrigues out of wedlock.

However, unexpected gifts of valuable property are among the possibilities; they will be inspired by some devoted affection; certainly, the financial affairs of the subject will be improved by people who love him; thus, an inheritance from a dear friend is indicated as probable.

If the subject's birth is "nocturnal," i. e., has taken place between the hours of midnight and noon, the sign of Taurus foretells that his father will be a man of some importance, either by his rank, by his fortune, or by his talents in art, literature, etc.

Brothers and sisters will be the causes of much serious trouble; the subject will have to take a very long journey on account of one of these blood relations.

Many travels are to be expected; if the

subject is born between midnight and noon, one of these journeys will prove very dangerous, perhaps fatal.

This sign must induce the subject to take great care of his children, especially his first-born; if it is a boy, he runs great dangers in his boyhood. Otherwise, the children will give great satisfaction and distinguish themselves, in a scientific career, at the bar, or in industrial pursuits. Still, the subject will have periods of sad disappointment with them.

The greater part of the subject's life will be peaceful and eventless; his main troubles will arise from difficulties the subject's inborn stubborness will cause him to create himself, or, at any rate, to magnify greatly.

This sign announces the following diseases as being in store for the subject: splenetic and plethoric troubles at 11, 23, 35 years of age. Besides, as the weak organs of the subject will be the kidneys and the liver, he must watch for the incipient symptoms of the stone and diseases of the spine. Let him beware of wounds from sharp instruments or from quadrupeds.

There is a sorrow or a death predicted, in relation with the subject's marriage.

While his position will be very modest in

his youth, he may reach great fortune and celebrity due to his talents in the line of the fine arts, or his discoveries in the realm of physics.

There will be many friends to brighten the life of the Taurus subject, but none of them of the steadfast kind, and most of them undesirable. Both the so-called friends and the subject's relatives will cause him many disappointments. The enmities he will encounter will be, fortunately, of the open kind, not of the hidden and treacherous variety.

The constellation Taurus always promises a long life, provided excesses of all kinds be avoided. The many perils through which the subject will pass, he may escape the worst consequences of, since they will be, so to speak, in full sight and known in advance.

The physical temperament of the Taurus subject will be bilious-sanguine in a southern latitude and lymphatic-nervous in a northern clime.

3. GEMINI. (The Twins.) ♊

The Constellation "Gemini"—the third of the Zodiac—exerts its influence from May 20 to June 18.

It endows the subject born during this period with probity, a pleasing, accommodating disposition, a temper quickly irritated but just as quickly calmed down, showing  but little violence in its outbursts and a great promptitude in manifesting repentance. The sign of Gemini often promises some kind of celebrity. It gives the subject natural, inventive genius, and, with it, a love of science for its own sake; it urges him to follow scientific researches, especially in the line of mathematics, and often makes him an orator or an author. It endows him, also, with some talents for commerce, with a saving disposition and moderation in the use of all things.

It renders him scrupulously honest, fairminded, and noble-hearted; he will possess a subtle, quick-seeing mind, an easy-flowing mode of speech; but the latter quality will manifest itself only when the subject is talking about some favorite topic of his; otherwise, he is rather reserved, even to taciturnity and often suffers strange perplexities and hesitations when the moment to act has arrived.

The expression of his will is firm, sometimes too affirmative, but without tyrannical tendencies, and without roughness.

Besides the scientific talents mentioned above, Gemini also gives a taste for fine arts, for music, especially the study of harmony, counterpoint, etc. In the scientific line, chemistry will be a prime favorite.

The wealth acquired by the practice of the talents above mentioned will lead the subject to many ups and downs, which, at times, will leave him almost in want, when, at other moments, his fortune will be quite large.

It will be the same as to the positions occupied by him; they will lack stability, now very brilliant, now again, of the humblest. These fluctuations will all be due to the subject's own acts.

This sign always foretells family secrets and family disagreements. Great trials will have to be gone through on account of, or caused by the subject's father.

Numerous will be the subject's children; some enmity will unfortunately be developed among them, and against their father or mother, or both.

The diseases that will be most threatening are bladder troubles, epidemic fevers, malaria; great perils will be incurred through quadrupeds, also from venomous bites and from enemies bent on serious mischief. The subject's family, his employes, or servants, will show themselves painfully and actively unfriendly toward him.

Great sorrows, troubles and disappointments will be caused by love affairs. There will be several marriages or long attachments in the subject's life.

He will have friends of all sorts and conditions, several of whom will turn his bitter enemies.

Toward middle life, he will meet with persistent obstacles to his success and legitimate promotion; they will be brought about by enmities to be found in the church or in the law profession. He will be to blame for the fact that these persons will be his enemies.

The position occupied by the subject and

constituting his life work will often be of a dual nature; he will constantly attempt to run two things at once; hence, many complications in his social relations. A disastrous betrayal is to be feared.

This sign foretells the existence of persistent, often armed enemies; the subject may even be waylaid. He will have cause to suspect his immediate associates, his relatives by marriage; he will suffer cruelly from tireless calumnies, from low intrigues relating to secrets in his family or that of his wife.

Gemini always announces events of a violent nature; but Providence may save the subject from their worst consequences.

The subject will have a sanguine-bilious constitution in a southern latitude, and a bilious-nervous temperament in a northern one.

4 CANCER. (The Crab.) ♋

The Constellation "Cancer"—the fourth of the Zodiac—exerts its influence from June 19 to July 23 (including the "5 Epagomenes," or supplementary degrees). It always gives to the subject a most agitated, restless existence, but a life of power and incessant activity.

Cancer endows the subjects it influences

with a taciturn disposition, with a searching mind and good morals, pure even to austerity. Their imagination, of a rich, creative character, will be in love with the fantastic;

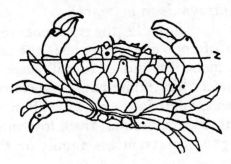

added to it will be a great aptitude for assimilation, so that the subject will be ever ready to act in real life the part of the particular hero for whom his imagination, his dreams, or his readings will have given him a temporary fancy.

The mood will be changeable, capricious, fickle to a degree, and the intercourse with others will suffer on that account, although the subject himself will not greatly care.

An unquenchable thirst for sympathy will make him attach himself to a new fancy as fast as the preceding one will lose its attraction.

This sign renders one discreet, independent, open-minded and versatile.

The Moon, who has its throne in this constellation, gives the subject sometimes the appearance of a most phlegmatic individual, and again it shows him up as a most unreasonably irritable fellow; both states of the mind are due to excessive impressionability and sensitiveness.

Those born under Cancer are quick in body and mind, clever in business matters and fit to command; they are ambitious to obtain wealth, honors and all the good things of life, and Cancer helps them to succeed, while it gives them decided religious tendencies. Women born under this sign are both hard workers and imperious. Eclecticism and general versatility are among the gifts of Cancer.

The complex influences that proceed from this sign, and which are more helpful to those who are born between midnight and noon, may render the subject either brave or cowardly according to circumstances and surroundings. The same individual may show himself one day suspicious or simply prudent to excess; and, the next morning, influenced by the phases of the moon, he may prove extravagantly thoughtless, absent-minded and fanciful.

These qualities are the causes of the sud-

den but weak and short-lived fits of anger of
the subject; in reality, it is only assumed
anger which will vanish like smoke.

Wealth will be often very hard to col-
lect, and the inherited patrimony may be
recklessly squandered, either by relatives or
by children of the subject.

Losses at the gaming table, or in speculation, or through thieves are to be expected;
but, in the latter part of life, the chances to
become rich are excellent.

During his youth, the subject will meet
with obstacles to his chosen vocation and
have troubles from near relations; he is
threatened with an early loss of brothers
or with quarrelling with them. He may
have a second (or adopted) family, outside
of his own. His children will cause him
much anxiety; it will be hard for him to
settle them in life, with the exception of the
eldest one, however, who will reach a high
position.

The subject's kindred will push him ener-
getically in the career he will finally select.

Many will be the vicissitudes and worries
of the subject; some of them of a mysterious
nature; but at the hour of most desperate
crisis, unexpected assistance will come up
providentially.

This sign gives one a repulsion against marriage and renders it, if entered into, quite unsatisfactory; the subject may inherit property from a first wife, but a law suit will be connected with it.

Travels will be long and profitable. One of them will make the subject comparatively famous and he will emerge "all right" out of the perils and struggles he may encounter in these journeys.

Some changes of residence will prove injurious to the health and to the pocket, on account of undesirable acquaintances or hidden enemies; even ambushes are to be feared, especially at he age of 14, 26 or 38.

Toward the 35th year the subject's position will be changed from good to bad or vice-versa. After that age it will be much more steady.

The subject will have many friends and protectors, especially among persons of the other sex; one of these patrons will run a great danger of total ruin, which will have a disastrous effect upon the subject.

At the age of 20, 32 and 44 there will be great peril resulting from secret intrigues of declared enemies or traitors among the subject's trusted friends.

Cancer generally gives the people born

under it excellent health. Should they be ill, the parts of the body to be affected will be the lungs and in general the breathing organs.

Wounds inflicted by the hands of man are foretold.

This sign gives the subject a lymphatic-bilious temperament in a southern climate and a lymphatic-nervous disposition in a northern latitude.

5. LEO. (The Lion.) ♌

The Constellation "Leo"—the fifth of the Zodiac—exerts its influence from July 24 to August 22.

Ptolemy, of Pelusa, surnamed the King of

Astrologers, said that the subjects born under this beneficent influence will reach positions of honor and trust.

Leo gives to those born under its influence a lofty mind, a spirit of fair play, an unbending dignity and a warm and generous heart. The will-power of the subject will be firm, enterprising and persevering; it will aim straight at the object desired, but secure it only by honest and above-board methods.

The mind will be steadfast, virile, proud, simple and liberal, with great brilliancy that may render it sometimes egotistic and presumptuous but never lacking in gratitude for an act of helpful kindness. The impulses and instincts will be always held within control. The temper will be kindly, though firm, courageous and magnanimous.

In the difficult moments of life, anger may be quickly aroused but it will harm no one and cool down almost at once.

Good will invariably be returned for evil; this will be the only kind of revenge practiced by the subject.

This sign induces one to love steadfastly; the affections will be constant, although forgetfulness may occur, in case of prolonged absence.

The special aptitudes of the subject will be of a soldierly character; he will be quite successful in all open-air sports, patient in all kinds of labor and admirably adapted to command. This sign does not endow the subject with many varied abilities, but those granted him will be of the best, often approaching perfection.

Leo gives a taste for pleasures and

luxury. Those born under this sign have nothing but disdain for the honors they are destined to reap almost without efforts.

The subject's inclinations will be strong, and yet well-reasoned out. His opinions will be fixed, passionate, sometimes exaggerated, and when he decides on a certain course of action he will follow it to the end, at all risks.

Those born under this sign will acquire, by their own merit, a good deal of property, besides what will come to them through relatives or influential friends. But their losses will be heavy and sudden, due to either gambling, or speculation, or imprudent loans; they may suffer from cruel spoliation, family property being taken from them quite unjustly. The death of a near relative will greatly compromise their pecuniary interests and their position; they will be shabbily treated in money matters by brothers and sisters, or other close relations. Even their parents may ruin their hopes of brilliant promotion.

During a short journey rendered necessary by the subject's position, he will have to fear some personal danger; the upper part of the body, the head and the shoulders especially, may be severely hurt.

Violent quarrels with relatives will be caused by a division of property or by family secrets, or by prolonged absence of the subject.

The father of the subject will be in peril of his life on a journey.

There will be many children coming to the subject who will have the sorrow of losing the eldest one.

If the subject is a woman she will probably be the mother of twins, or she may have children of two successive husbands; when these children will be grown up, they will give her trouble.

Long and complicated diseases are threatening; the woman born under Leo will have great troubles in, and resulting from, child-birth. Servants and employes of the subject will be the cause of constant worries.

Leo always announces family disagreements.

Several unforeseen legacies, or even inheritances, will render easier the circumstances of the subject and especially of his children who often will be the beneficiaries; there is a probability, however, that relatives may succeed in diverting these wind-falls away from the subject and his family.

The subject will make but few sea voyages; the first one will be detrimental to his interests and a source of losses.

His position will demand frequent voyages on land; one of these will prove highly advantageous and bring about a sudden change for the better.

The offices coming to the subject will be offices of great honor but small emoluments; he may grievously compromise his chances in that direction, or even forfeit these valued prizes, in an instant, by some most unfortunate and thoughtless moves.

He will enjoy some reputation, even marked celebrity, through his own merit and without the help of any outside protection. It may be in the sciences, or the fine arts that he will find his true sphere and make a shining success. As said above, the ruin of these promising prospects will be due either to an unfortunate voyage or to a rash act on the part of the subject.

His friends will be many, but of little assistance, even if their fortune and position be such as to give them the means to be of great use; on the contrary, they will probably cause the subject some heavy financial losses.

His few enemies will be declared ones;

low and cowardly intrigues against him will prove so invariably unsuccessful, that he will soon be free from such attacks.

Leo gives those born under it a nervous-sanguine temperament, a remarkably fine health and a long life.

However, the subject may be attacked by inflammatory rheumatism, located especially in the knees. Pneumonia, and in general, troubles of the respiratory organs, and troubles of the spleen and the bladder are also among the possibilities; wounds, if any, will affect the feet and hands.

According to the old astrologers, Leo, containing the throne of the Sun, is always the prognostic of a fine fortune and a lofty position.

6 VIRGO. (The Virgin.) ♍

The Constellation of "Virgo"—the sixth of the signs of the Zodiac—exerts its influence from August 23 to September 21.

Those born within this period will reach honors through their personal merit.

This sign bestows on them a cool reason, a spirit of equity, a merciful disposition and a taste for everything that is honest and straightforward.

The moral nature of the subject will be

mild, modest, amiable, confiding, and yet not easily fathomed.

His will-power, although comparatively firm may be influenced through sentimental motives.

He will be intelligent, ingenious, but above all, moved by his feelings to which he will remain passionately attached. He will be slow to anger and slow to quiet down, although his wrath will never harm any one. He will be moved to repentance quickly and deeply. Virgo gives people born under it a taste for cloister life, a love of divine thoughts; or, in a lower plane, an inclination toward the liberal arts and the gift of persuasive eloquence.

To the taste for art the subject will add a liking for agriculture or horticulture and a

mild mania for collecting things. He will
show a real aptitude for the higher sciences
and deeper studies. All his tastes will be
under his control and his opinions easily
changed.

Those born under Virgo run serious
physical dangers from their earliest babyhood and all through childhood.

It is almost an invariable fact that they
will have the greatest difficulty to acquire
even moderate means, and this small competence will be constantly threatened, during the first part of their lives. Later, they
will be luckier financially and recover some
family property.

Although this sign foretells wealth, due to
the hard work and intelligence of the subject applied in the field of science and art,
or through successful inventions, or thanks
to some high office connected with the
Church, still, by the fault of the subject
himself, there is a strong probability of his
losing suddenly that (either mcney or position) which he will have acquired through
such long and laborious efforts.

Travels may be the cause of some large
addition to the subject's fortune.

Relatives, near or distant, will prove
rather harmful than otherwise.

The subject may have many brothers and sisters, but there will be no harmony between them, and he will lose several of them at an early age, probably in a violent manner.

There will be sad and grave family secrets, either on account of irregular unions, or through divorces or separations.

There is here a prognostic of sudden losses of children, either through a fall from a high place, or through drowning, or through quadrupeds.

Virgo always announces some violent happenings, great obstacles in love matters, serious law suits, dissensions between friends or relatives, between husband and wife, even divorces. Let us say here that "unions and marriages" are expressed by the same indications in astrology, and must be understood aright by the parties interested.

The struggle for life will be particularly hard for those born under this sign. But, after painful efforts, and many disappointments, the subjects of Virgo generally triumph. "Better late than never," ought to be their motto.

They will have decided religious tendencies.

The Virgo subject will have a chance to marry twice. But his second union will be

the cause of a great upheaval in his existence; it may be for his good, and again it
may prove disastrous.

Few inheritances will come the way of
the subject; those that will be within his
reach will be acquired only after long and
disagreeable law proceedings.

The subject may have to undertake,
generally against his will, long travels,
either to try his fortune in a foreign country or to fill a mission of importance with, or
in obedience to, the orders of some great man.
But travel he will, surely and frequently.

It will be a hard pull for him to succeed,
since he will have only his own self to depend upon; but he will succeed and reach a
high position in the world. He may even
acquire riches through his intelligence and
activity; but if he does get wealthy, it will
be on account of the dangerous profession
or occupation he will have selected. It may
be the result of perilous experimenting in
the realm of physics, for which he will be
particularly well adapted.

His friends will be very few, very uncer-
tain and of little use to him; a few pleasant
acquaintances, met in his travels, will be
among the least undesirable of his associates; but he will soon lose track of them.

The subject will have secret enemies in the world of art, or in the financial marts, or among business leaders; they will cause him numerous, heavy losses, especially through bad investments.

In southern climates, Virgo gives those born under it a lymphatic-bilious temperament; in northern climates, their consitution will be lymphatic-nervous. The weaker spots will be the stomach, the liver and the legs.

7. LIBRA. (The Balance.) ♎

This Constellation, "Libra"—the seventh of the signs of the Zodiac—also called "the Scales"—exerts its influence from September 22 to October 21.

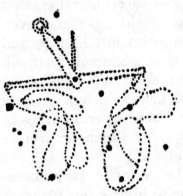

It endows those born under its influence with great gentleness, straightforwardness and pure moral principles; it renders the soul merciful and the heart affectionate and constant.

The disposition is frank, open, confiding,

slightly melancholy; anger is easily aroused and rapidly quieted down again.

This sign causes indecision in opinions and in actions; it bestows upon one inventive genius, a special aptitude for mechanical arts and sciences and for navigation; but all these gifts will not profit the subject.

The will-power, although plentiful, knows not how to bring about final results.

The subjects of Libra are prone to study, handy with tools as well as quick at figures, but care little for the fine arts, except music, being devoted, heart and soul, to business. Otherwise, in the choice of their pleasures, they show refinement.

Their passions are deep and honest.

They are changeable in their opinions, although strongly attached—for a time—to the idea or theory that rules over them temporarily.

Toward the middle of his life, the subject born under Libra will make a fortune, thanks to some industry connected with navigation, or at least with water as motive-power. He will have to defend his wealth in court; a great law suit which he will ultimately win, will create bitter enmities, perhaps even a serious disagreement between him and his spouse or partner.

He will have many brothers and sisters, some of them by a second wife of the father or by a second husband of the mother; these blood relations will be constantly at odds between themselves and with the subject.

He may have some trouble with his parents, especially with his father, who will lack the paternal fiber. If the subject is born between noon and midnight there is a risk of his losing his father early in life.

Few children will come to him, and one of them will be the cause of great anxieties.

Family relations will be frequently disturbed; there is a prognostic of a second family, perhaps an adopted one; or the subject himself may be the object of adoption.

Diseases characterized by a flow of some kind are to be expected; the weak organs of those born under Libra are the bowels and the bladder. The hands and feet are threatened with wounds.

The sign which presides over marriage, in the arrangement of the Zodiacal Constellations, is "Aries" in House VII. It is fickle, violent in temper, and barren; it is directly opposed to Libra, but unsatisfactory as this opposition is, the subject will gain riches through marriage. Through the

death of the spouse he will make a large inheritance totally unexpected.

Those born under this sign had better beware of sea voyages; they will prove dangerous and never profitable.

Toward middle age, there is a threat of loss of position, and a warning that the mother of the subject may be the cause, direct or indirect, of this disastrous happening.

The subject has in prospect the probabilities of reaching some high and honored position; his relatives will assist him in his ambitions; he will possess protectors and friends among the great people of this world; they will show themselves steadfast, assist him to a brilliant marriage, lend him their moral and material support in matters of business; and yet, it will come to pass, that, willingly, or not, the subject will do grievous harm to one of these powerful friends.

He will meet with serious enmity on the part of certain clergymen on account of family matters; other enemies will come up among lawyers and men of learning.

An ancient tradition says that the persons born under this sign will be the cause of their own troubles and perhaps of their death.   In southern latitudes the subjects of Libra are naturally sanguine-bilious; in northern climates they are nervous-bilious.

8. SCORPIO. (The Scorpion.) ♏

This Constellation, "Scorpio"—the-eighth of the Zodiac—exerts its influence from October 22 to November 20.

It endows the subject born during this period with a mind at the same time

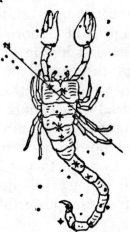

shrewd, persuasive, fickle, capricious, dreamy, poetical and often religiously inclined.

He has a firm hold upon himself and his will-power is steadfast and persevering.

The temper is fiery, bellicose and easily aroused, somewhat rough and even violent, but never unkindly so; there is a love of danger for its own sake. This sign renders those born under it phlegmatic, taciturn and close mouthed; they are often tinged with misanthropy.

Slow to move to anger, they are also slow to forgive; they keep a deep feeling of resentment, and as their wrath cools down it becomes almost more dangerous, for in their revengeful spirit, they are relentless and act quickly and recklessly.

If the phlegmatic tendency is the predominant symptom, they oppose their adversary by the mere force of inertia.

If they are not toned down by education and proper surroundings, the subjects of Scorpio are quarrelsome and fond of seeking trouble with or without cause.

This constellation renders those born under it skillful and patient in all kinds of work; it gives them a love for architecture, for simple country pleasures, and withal, a thirst for honors.

In their opinions they are stubborn, rarely amenable to reason and disagreeably aggressive.

This sign gives little prosperity in the first part of life, but promises plenty of it in mature years. Unexpected gains will accrue at that time of life; they may come from matters connected with religious worship or be the result of long journeys; an inheritance is also among the most serious probabilities. Scorpio always brings fortune in its train.

The subject will have few brothers if **any;**

one of them is threatened with a fatal accident either through a fall or through drowning.

If the subject is born between midnight and noon his father will suffer complete ruin in his position and fortune.

Scorpio always gives to his subjects a numerous progeny.

Malignant fevers contracted across the sea will threaten the subject's life; he will also suffer from constant headaches and cruel fits of neuralgia; through excesses of some kind—work or dissipation—a severe illness will come, but recovery is possible.

The subject will surely marry, in fact, he will marry twice as an early widowhood is foretold; one of these unions will be unfortunate. Either of the spouses will be in slight danger of being crippled by a large quadruped, by secret enemies or by accident.

Deep heart-sorrows will come to the subject by the early loss (before the age of thirty), of a dearly loved one, either wife or husband or sweetheart, or friend of either sex.

Long journeys will be undertaken over land and sea; they will not be particularly fortunate.

As success will come to him comparatively late in life, he will have passed middle life before he tastes a secure peace, bitterly fought for through a laborious youth.

Many will be his friends, and the kindly favors of the great will not be wanting; but one friend or protector will be the cause of great trouble in the march of success, or in a love affair.

Enmities will also be numerous and they will stick to the subject the best part of his life. These will be found even among his daily associates, both social and in business.

If the subject visits a foreign country, he will be in great danger of being waylaid; but he will escape scot free, as all those born under Scorpio are singularly well protected against accidents or attacks.

In warm climates the subjects of Scorpio are lymphatic-bilious, in cold latitudes they are nervous-bilious.

9. SAGITTARIUS.   (The Archer.) ♐

This Constellation, "Sagittarius" — the ninth sign of the Zodiac—exerts its influence from November 21 to December 20.

It endows those born during this period with an ingenuous, strictly honest nature, with a generous heart, that does kindly acts

without a thought of reward or even gratitude.

The ancient Magi claimed that the subjects of Sagittarius would prove exception-
ally good, or radically bad.

The mind of the subject is versatile, gentle, easy-going, peaceable; quick to anger
 and quicker to qui-
et down, very lib-
eral and impartial
,in his opinions, and
.with a gift for
rapid assimilation.
But it worries a
great deal about
trifles and shows
anxiety out of pro-
portion with the trouble in prospect. The
temper does not grow heated, except when
unjustly attacked, or if placed in the presence of dangerous people.

The subject of Sagittarius has an extremely sensitive and nervous disposition,
and, on that account, shows, at times, an
irritability only skin-deep, however, and of
short duration. Otherwise he is habitually
cheerful, often like a child.

Sagittarius gives simplicity, and uncon-
ventionality, and an intense love of inde-

pendence.   Its subjects are always on their guard over themselves and over others, although frequently deceived, just the same; they love harmony and prefer giving way rather than fight and win.   Their extreme timidity prevents them often from asserting their rights, but at times they suddenly conquer it and show that they are no cowards. They are not easily understood as they keep much to themselves.   They are skillful with their hands and arc gifted with eloquence; the fine arts and certain branches of science attract them; they love solitude, and study by themselves behind locked doors.

Their passions are fully under control, and yet they are ardent and numerous; their opinions are always moderate, rather of an eclectic nature and frequently changed.

The subjects of Sagittarius will be in poor circumstances in infancy and childhood, on account of losses their parents will have suffered from.

Their personal merits will assist them in building a fortune to which a few legacies will be added later.

This sign announces that the subjects will have few brothers and sisters, and that they will not be on good terms with them;

one of them will die an early death **or** barely escape.

On account of certain family secrets, a serious disagreement will intervene between the subject and his parents, or parents-in-law, or step-parents. He will have but few children and the eldest one will be a cause of serious worry; in fact, he will not get along with his children and they will live away from him.

This sign foretells two marriages, one of which will be of great detriment to the subject's position.

The aptitudes as well as the occupations will be of two different kinds, interfering greatly with each other, and thus hindering success. The subject will have reached middle age before obtaining the position and fortune due to him on account of his talents.

He will suffer from frequent minor physical ailments, such as sore-throat, sick headaches, etc. Until his thirtieth year he will meet with frequent falls from high places.

Many long journeys, but none by water, will be made necessary by his position and his business. During one of these trips, he will hear of the death of a near relative.

Socially he will meet with success and make many friends, one of whom will prove treacherous and almost bring about the loss of the subject's position. He will have protectors of high degree, among them a person of lofty standing, who will be extremely useful to him at a critical moment.

His enemies will show themselves bitter and persistent; they will not hesitate to slander him cruelly, and try their best to ruin his prosperity in business and in love

This constellation gives to its subjects a purely nervous temperament in Southern climates, and a nervous-bilious disposition in Northern latitudes. It promises them a long life.

10. CAPRICORN. (The Sea-Goat.) ♑

This Constellation, "Capricorn" —the tenth sign of the Zodiac—exerts its influence from December 21 to January 19.

The persons born under its influence will be self-made men, the builders of their own fortune, and they will know how to remain prosperous.

Capricorn also endows its subjects with a strong taste for destroying things, an active disposition, a vigorous body, especially if born between midnight and noon, for, if born between noon and midnight they may have a few physical defects and suffer from accidents. They will show themselves aggressive, warlike, enthusiastic, vehement, and yet, inclined to melancholy and saving habits.

Their mind will be shrewd, fair and clever in business matters, and decidedly versatile.

Their will-power, although strong, may vary in its object, but will finally succeed in reaching the desired goal.

Capricorn renders its subjects rather brusque in their manners, with such decided ways that they will often seem rude. They will be slow to anger and slow to forgive, although they do not harbor mean, revengeful feelings.

They are very prudent and circumspect, never making a move without lengthy deliberation.

Capricorn endows those born under it with quickness and agility and with a sound eyesight.

They will not prove constant in love matters, although this fickleness may be frequently caused by the influence of others, not by an inborn unfaithful disposition.

Money will come to the subject through his own talents and efforts, seldom through gifts or inheritance.

Brothers and sisters will be numerous, but harmful rather than helpful.

The Capricorn subject will undertake many short journeys, several of them in consequence of his enemies' intrigues.

His father will make him suffer through his violence; his family will be a source of more trouble than satisfaction; they will interfere with his matrimonial projects.

In his youth, he will have to face great physical dangers, either wounds in war or severe illnesses.

This constellation is not prolific; it is better so, since the children of the subject, if he has any, will ruin his position or his conduct will ruin the children's lives.

Great struggles are foretold; difficult and mysterious intrigues developing during journeys or on account of them; clerical gentlemen will be mixed in the matter. Until the subject has passed his 42d year he will have to undergo many vicissitudes and be ill-treated by relatives.

The Capricorn subjects suffer greatly

from gout, rheumatism in the joints, especially in the arms and hands; they are troubled also with certain stomach disorders. They may expect bruises due to falls; they will develop a tendency to hypochondria.

The marriage question is in their case both serious and complex. The Cancer constellation, whose part it is to preside over alliances between sexes, is particularly fickle and changeable; it is in direct opposition to Capricorn, which it, therefore, greatly influences, and so the subjects of the latter will meet with serious troubles in their marital relations, and will probably marry more than once.

Capricorn interferes sadly with long journeys, and renders them quite dangerous, either through accidents, or through severe illnesses or wounds.

There will be more than one Judas Iscariot among the friends of the subject; his position will run great risks through their dark intrigues. A powerful protection will help the subject upward, especially if he has chosen the army or navy as his career.

He will meet two kinds of enemies; some in high places, others low down in social rank; his brothers and sisters (at least one of them) will not prove his friends. Finally, he will triumph over all this active or latent ill-will, or it will subside of itself.

The Capricorn constellation gives its subjects a lymphatic-nervous physical temperament in Southern climes, and a lymphatic-bilious disposition in Northern latitudes.

11. AQUARIUS. (The Water-Bearer.) ♒

This Constellation, "A q u a r i u s"—the eleventh sign of the Zodiac—exerts its influence from January 20 to February 18.

It endows the persons born under it with a special aptitude for the fine arts and secures popular recognition for their remarkable works. Besides, it gives them a long life and lofty position, and makes of them orators and authors.

However, t h e y will have none but t h e m s e l v e s to blame if they are persecuted or even exiled.

They will have graceful, gentle, simple, and straightforward natures. Although violent when driven to wrath, they quiet down quickly and bear no grudge.

The will-power will be firm, but lacking in logic and be apt to rush to its goal unmindful of obstacles over which it will ride rough shod. The Aquarius subjects will be fond of solitude, laborious and diligent, patient and persevering. They are well endowed for serious studies, and for ruling over other people; they are always dreaming of riches and honors.

Passionate in all their undertakings, their opinions are ardent, steadfast and strongly convincing.

The property the subject will acquire will not be permanently in his possession, but be taken from him repeatedly through the intrigues of evil-minded people, some of them his pretended friends, who will, at times, resort to violence to deprive him of his own. Through members of his family he will come to much money, but other blood relations will damage his position and reputation.

The Aquarius subjects will be great travelers, sometimes against their will; but these journeys will generally turn out badly and interfere disastrously with the financial prospects and the social position of the subjects; their health also will suffer on that account.

They will have few brothers and sisters, if any; they will receive from them little else but unpleasant, even cruel, treatment.

On a short trip, the subject will run some serious bodily risk, probably on the water or through fire-arms or quadrupeds.

His father will die of sudden death, or meet with unexpected financial reverses. Scientific researches may be the cause of either disaster.

Aquarius subjects are often blessed with twins. Death in child-birth is among the probabilities; the infants that will come to them will be delicate in health and hard to raise.

Among diseases that will afflict them are troubles of the stomach and the lungs, violent sick headaches and brain neuralgia.

The Constellation Leo, in whose resort all unions between sexes are placed, foretells for the Aquarius subjects a marriage with an artist, actor or professional musician.

The career of the subject will be full of ups and downs, the latter often of the most disheartening kind; but he will always come

3

out a victor, either through his unfaltering efforts, or through the opportune assistance of his friends.

For his friends will be many and really devoted. People in high position will contribute to the subject's final triumph over his difficulties.

But his enemies also will be many and relentless, using both hidden and open, violent means to undo him; he will conquer them through a series of almost providential circumstances.

Still the risks ahead of him are many, mostly due to his own rashness and his ruinous love of change. His friends will often quarrel with him on that account. But Aquarius will bestow upon him public esteem, and the kindly advice of the wise will help him to reach a pre-eminent position among his fellow-citizens.

Those born under this constellation have a bilious-sanguine temperament in Southern climes, and a nervous-sanguine physical disposition in Northern latitudes.

12. PISCES. (The Fishes.) ♓

This Constellation, "Pisces"—the twelfth sign of the Zodiac—exerts its influence from February 10 to March 20.

Those born under this sign will be the artisans of their own celebrity and will attain it in the realm of the fine arts, sciences or literature. Popularity will come to them unbidden, as a reward of unwearying efforts in developing their natural talents.

Pisces endows its subjects with a certain degree of restlessness, with a constant dis-

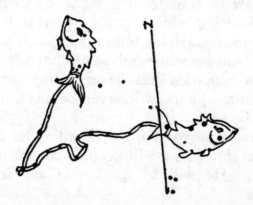

position to find fault with the results of their own labor, thus inciting them to further efforts; they are somewhat pessimistic and inclined to alter their views to reach the goal more rapidly. They have a kind of duplex moral nature difficult to fathom, but withal strictly honest, fair in all its dealings, poetical, dreamy and mystical.

The morals of the subject will be pure, owing to his high principles, for he will

otherwise be very fond of pleasure. **He**
will be of a proud disposition and that will
keep him away from anything degrading.

His will is strong while it lasts; but it will
change its object frequently; he will be
mildly despotic, without a real tyrannical
trait.

His prudence will be remarkable; he will
be slow to confide in any one, or to make
real friends, while always cheerful in his
relations toward his fellow beings.

He will be witty and somewhat sarcastic
in his remarks, but never biting or unpleasant. There will never be any sting in
what he says.

Slow to move to anger, he will quiet down
just as slowly, but will keep no rancor in his
heart. He will be quick, vigilant, indus-
trious.

This constellation gives those born under
it gifts of eloquence in speech and writing,
and causes them to love a generous diet,
especially when sitting with friends around
a well-laden board. It will make them
sociable to a marked degree.

Their opinions will be ardent, but rather
eclectic than one-sided.

By his work, by his personal merit, the
subject of Pisces will be able to acquire

wealth; but he will be kept poor by imprudent alliances or reckless speculations.

Generally, this sign foretells two or more
professions, pursued simultaneously or suc-
cessively, as the subject will prove remarkably versatile.

He will have more sisters than brothers,
and will lose one of them early in life. His
parents had to suffer from serious mishap
or losses during his childhood.

This twelfth constellation generally promises its subjects many travels and plenty of
money, although the ownership of the family estate may be contested in law by step-
father or step-mother, on account of a
second marriage of the subject's surviving
parent.

He will leave the family home at an early
age, while his people will not be great
travelers.

This constellation announces two marriages for the subject, one with a widow or
widower; there will be some misfortune connected with either the first or the second
spouse; the other marriage will be a very
happy one.

Severe accidents will happen in his family.
He will undertake many journeys; their
object will be the acquiring of fortune, or

reputation, or both. He will change his residence and maybe his position, very frequently.

Pisces promises those born under it, high public or social positions and the favor of people of lofty standing—probably a liberal profession as one's life's work and sometimes two distinct careers.

The illnesses peculiar to this sign are fevers and troubles of the heart or eyes; the accidents that may occur will be of trifling nature. Unpleasant dreams will annoy the subject.

Besides a few solid friendships, the subject will have very treacherous friends, one in particular whose odious conduct toward him will almost wreck his life.

Many will be the envious ones whose occult or open intrigues will have to be constantly guarded against. They will fail in their evil designs, unless the subject's conduct be such as to give them a serious hold upon his destiny.

In Southern climes, the subjects of Pisces are by nature lymphatic-bilious; in Northern latitudes, they are lymphatic-nervous.

CONCLUSION OF THE INTERPRETATION OF THE
SIGNS OF THE ZODIAC.

We are compelled to admit that a hasty
perusing of characteristics thus assigned by
tradition to the subjects of the various
Zodiacal signs, may reveal a number of discouraging contradictions, at least on the
surface, until the student has fairly grasped
the onward, esoteric significance of these
long enumerations of qualities, defects,
probable accidents, etc.

This unfavorable impression disappears,
however, as soon as one takes the trouble
to classify these various "symptomatic
prophesies," according to the *Trinary
Kabbalistic divisions*, or "*Trinocracies*," the
importance of which cannot be too strongly
insisted upon.

As I mentioned repeatedly in my large
book on Palmistry* all visible manifestations
of the occult may, or rather, *must*, bear
three distinct separate meanings, to be used,
the one or the other, or again the third,
according to the elements in the human
being which we wish to understand and
fathom.

---

* *The Study of Palmistry for Professional Purposes
and for Advanced Pupils.* Large 8vo vol. of 480 pp., and
1,251 illustrations.

We have:

First: The World of the *Soul—Inspira-tion.*

Second: The World of the *Mind—Intellect.*

Third: The World of *Matter—Action.*

To the *first world* belong religious and psychological aspirations, the knowledge of good and evil, Conscience.

To the *second world* belong: Imagination at its best, or its worst; what is erroneously called Genius; the gift of reasoning, of higher eloquence, of poetry, of art, of music, the inventive faculty, the direct influence over one's fellow beings.

Finally, to the *third world:* Our passions, our instincts, our love for doing and undo-ing, the creative or destructive impulses.

Now that we have laid down, in a few brief words, the tripartite rule that must govern our investigations, of ourselves or other human beings, be it by Astrology, Chiromancy, Graphology, or Phrenology, let the student read over the special charac-teristics (given above) that have been, from prehistoric times to our days, attributed to those born under this or that sign of the Zodiac, and he will have no difficulty to find his way through what appeared at first a rather inextricable labyrinth.

Should he desire, however, to plunge a little further into the mysteries of the *three worlds*, inasmuch as this classification enters into the scheme of this work, he may read the following pages, that will, doubtless, lighten the wide stretches of kabbalistic horizon still left dark in this our popular exposition of the particularities of the Zodiac subjects.

THE FOUR TYPICAL TEMPERAMENTS

BILIOUS: Dark complexion, strong muscles, great vitality, strong passions, tenacity of purpose.

SANGUINE: Brilliant complexion, active mind and body, energy, fickleness of purpose.

NERVOUS: Delicate features, rapid circulation of blood, irritability of vital functions and temper, shrewdness.

LYMPHATIC: Flabby muscles, dull complexion, sluggish of circulation, emotion and mind.

As the pure type is rarely found, a temperament is best described by modifying one of the above terms by another. George Washington might be called sanguine-bilious; Victor Hugo, nervous-sanguine.

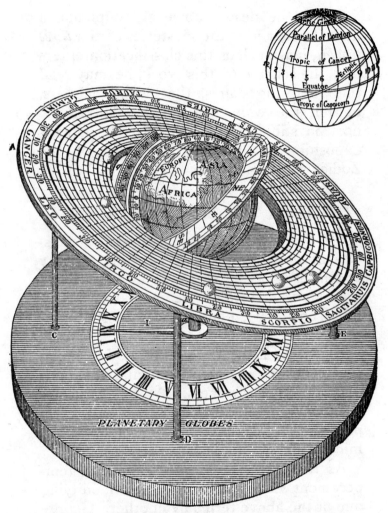

An ancient instrument demonstrating the distance of the planets from the earth and the plane of their paths. The smaller cut represents the earth, its zones, equator, etc.

CHAPTER IV

THE PLANETS

In the first two chapters we have completed what is called "the Orientation of a Horoscope," meaning by this the position of the Sun on the Ecliptic on the day of birth of any one whose life we propose studying. Of course, without this exact date, nothing can be done toward the casting of a Horoscope, but, on the other hand, astrological readings, to be reliable and truly personal, depend on other facts and calculations which will be gradually unfolded to the reader. Horoscopes based solely on Zodiacal indications have a real, intrinsic value and one of the most popular books in America claims that they include everything worth knowing in this order of ideas.

But the details of one's life, i. e., information about Health, Fortune and Love, are not convincingly and accurately revealed by the signs of the Zodiac, studied singly and by themselves.

Although I have neither the space nor the inclination, in these short and practical lessons, to attempt a defence, or simply an explanation, of the mysteries of ancient Astrology, I must state the following as an article of faith in astrological researches.

In this great Universe, all the realms, all the Worlds, are included in a huge solidarity, just as in our little bit of a world the various elements, whether endowed with life or not, all depend on each other and are the component parts of a great whole. If this be so—and this primordial law is being made clearer and more certain every day by the discoveries of modern science—the larger celestial orbs or luminaries exert a most decided influence over us—the Earth —just as we, ourselves, do exert an influence over them.

In my first chapter I named "seven" celestial bodies, which have been recognized from all antiquity as the bestowers of powerful fluidic influence over our planet. In the order of their nearness to us they are:

Between us and the Sun: Venus and Mercury.

Farther from the Sun than the Earth: Mars, Jupiter and Saturn.

To these five planets let us add: The Sun itself, and the Moon, which, as we all know, is a satellite of the Earth.

Now, to each of these five Planets have been assigned by tradition a Throne by day and a Residence by night, in one of the signs of the Zodiac. The illustration used in this chapter places the symbols of these planets where they belong, that is:

SATURN by day—in Aquarius; by night—in Capricorn.

JUPITER by day—in Sagittarius; by night—in Pisces.

MARS by day—in Aries; by night—in Scorpio.

VENUS by day—in Libra; by night—in Taurus.

MERCURY by day—in Gemini; by night—in Virgo.

The SUN is, day and night, in Leo, while the MOON is, night and day, in Cancer.

Remember, these are the specially elected Dwellings of the seven Planets, and their meanings are to be understood in connection with the readings we have given of the signs of the Zodiac. This adds that much more precision to the information we have already gathered from the signs themselves and "by themselves."

But before giving these meanings, and describing the human types that bear, as it were, the visible imprint of the particular

Planets exerting upon them a predominating influence, let me state at once that the main study of the would-be astrologer, professional or amateur, is to learn how to

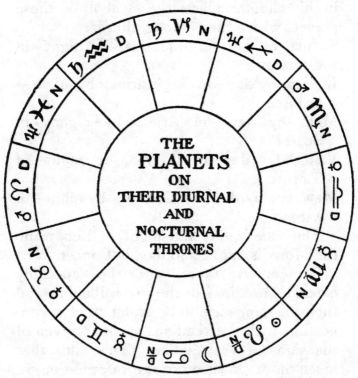

THE PLANETS ON THEIR DIURNAL AND NOCTURNAL THRONES

locate exactly the position of each of these Planets, on the day, and, if possible, the hour, of birth of the person whose horoscope is being cast. This has always been considered as the most difficult part of the cast-

ing process and arduous mathematical operations have been claimed to be indispensable to reach this result with any degree of accuracy.

If you have perused other works on Astrology, you are aware that they require calculations about the moon's position, the planets' *declinations*, etc. To avoid this difficulty I have spent years in hard work, until now I shall be able, in my concluding lesson, to give the student a much simpler and most accurate system for putting together the different elements of a Horoscope, all of which we shall have, by that time, thoroughly mastered together. But this is anticipating and getting away from the subject of this lesson, the Planets.

Of the seven celestial orbs, Saturn, Mars and, often, the Moon, are considered as decidedly unfavorable or "inimical." The Sun, Venus and Jupiter, on the other hand, are constantly favorable or "friendly." Mercury is sometimes good, sometimes bad. Of course, their positions, on the day of the subject's birth, not only influence the said subject's whole life, but also react upon each other and, in that way, modify greatly the meanings of each separate orb, and the type it represents on Earth.

1. SATURN

Any one born under this Planet will be, in physical appearance, unprepossessing and even somewhat repulsive. The complexion is dull; the hair is straight, dark and dull and is lost early. Their teeth, also, are poor. They walk with a stoop and with eyes downcast; they are awkward and fall frequently; they are often deaf and suffer from rheumatism. They are skeptics born, even scoffers, and have no liking for the society of their fellow beings. Among them are found poisoners, anarchists and all sorts of public and private enemies. They are fond of the wicked sides of the occult sciences, of chemistry, agriculture and mining; they are misers at heart, and smile but rarely. Saturn has a disastrous influence upon the nervous system and drives one to insanity. The Saturnians, as they are called, are born gamblers and unlucky ones at that.

2. JUPITER

This Planet—next in size and nearness to the Sun—endows those born under its influence—Jupiterians—with a handsome, most pleasing physique, and a most cheerful, jovial disposition. They are general favorites, in fact, too much so, for their own good, as they have a tendency to live too high and too fast. They have a clear, somewhat florid complexion and a disposition to stoutness. Their hair is plentiful and curly, they lose it early in life. Their teeth are good, sometimes a little large in front; they often have dimples. They are great lovers of comforts; their ambition is generally successful, doubtless on account of their popularity due to the pleasant magnetism that emanates from them. In religion, they love everything that appeals to their senses; they are most of the time in love but are more sensual than truly affectionate. At bottom, and unless otherwise influenced, they are weak and lack the power to resist temptation. In its best type, the Jupiterian (or "Jovial") is magnanimous, noble-hearted and a born leader of men—or women.

3. MARS

Between Jupiter and the Earth, Astronomy places the Planet Mars, with which it is claimed we are about to communicate by means of electric waves. Whether such result be obtainable or not, it is certain that the majority of human beings born under the influence of Mars—the Martians (or

"Martials")—are heavily built but physically strong. They are not gifted with much intellectuality and care but little for any form of learning, except as it refers to out-door sports, travels in dangerous countries and military affairs. They are brave to a degree, only too ready to risk their lives for little or no purpose; they are easily angered, and, for the time being, forget everything in the excess of their violence. The worst Martian type will commit murder before he knows it. At their best, those born under Mars will show themselves straightforward and incapable of any kind of fraud. Their word is their bond and they are ready for hard work. They are patient, faithful and true, but not "brainy." A male Martian is generally a great favorite with the ladies and is apt to be rather quick and unscrupulous in his courtship methods. He is not a sentimental lover. A bad Martian is a loud. fatiguing talker and a braggard.

Now we have studied the Astrological meanings of the three Planets placed, in the Solar system, farther from the Sun than we —the Earth—are. Between us and the Sun we find, first:

4. VENUS

This is one of the most favorable or "friendly" Planets. The persons born under its influence have many physical, mental and moral traits in common with those born under Jupiter. But the Venusians—it is the name they are known by in Astrological lore—possess a more effeminate style of beauty and their general temperament is also cast somewhat in the same molds; thus, their complexion is ultra-clear and their skin very thin and transparent. Their height is below the average; the face full, the forehead smooth but often too narrow for perfect beauty; the hair is dark with a brilliant shine, the eyebrows and lashes are gracefully pencilled. The nose is fleshy and the nostrils dilate whenever a pleasure is in prospect; the eyes are smiling and bathed in a tender languor; frequently one eye is larger than the other. The mouth is small, with full lips of a bright red; it displays white and perfect teeth and coral-red gums, The body is plump but beautifully shaped, with no bone prominent; the hips are rather too marked. Hands and feet are small and well formed. Venusians are found of dress, of jewelry, of flowers, of perfumes, of music—especially simple, melodious music. They are often quite expert in some of the fine arts, which they cultivate more for the pleasure they find in them and to charm their friends than for the satisfaction of their vanity or for profit. The Venusians are remarkable for their constant good humor and their aversion to all strife and quarreling, even of the mildest character. They generally have large families. If this planet be under unfavorable aspects from Saturn, or Mars, its best benefits turn into terrible defects, especially if Jupiter is also in bad aspects. Then the effeminacy grows to such an extent as to destroy every noble trait in the subject's nature; the inherent sensuality of the Venusian allowing itself unrestricted scope becomes the cause of gravest excesses and ruins the subject's prospects. Sometimes, if the Venusian be a man and Mars should react on Venus, brutality in love matters will be the dominant feature of the wretched victim of this sad combination. As a matter of fact, in the good as well as in the bad Venusian, the senses are all powerful; they may act in a more refined way in the first case than in the second, but in either case, they have still to be watched over closely or may turn out to be rather unreliable rulers.

5. MERCURY

As I stated above, Mercury is an unclassified Planet, a sort of "free lance," in the Astrological world. It is at times "friendly," at others decidedly "inimical." It all depends upon the aspect of the other planets toward it. Those born under Mercury—the Mercurians as they are called—are small in stature, but remarkable for their agility and bodily skill. Mentally, they are endowed with a versatility which renders them apt to undertake almost any study, trade, or profession, and make a success of it. They remain young-looking very late in life and their complexion, rather of a creamy white, is often tinted by blushes. The hair is chestnut-colored and curls at the end; the forehead is high, the eyebrows meet, the eyes themselves are deep-set and penetrating, a little too restless, perhaps; the nose is straight, the upper lip protrudes slightly; the chin is long and pointed.

The Mercurians are active to a degree, fond of money-making and clever in business. Their voice is not strong and yet they are often eloquent, but of an eloquence that does not dazzle; it is of a convincing, not of a showy, style. They are born logicians and, on that account, are excellent mathematicians; they have wit, are quick at repartee and excel in turning a threatening failure into success. They are met most frequently among the professions, the medical particularly; they are successful in society and a Mercurian of the fair sex has always a crowd of fascinated admirers in her train when much handsomer women remain uncourted. In fact, adventurers of both sexes are, eight times out of ten, Mercurians, for they need a great deal of personal magnetism to victimize their dupes. Affected by Saturn, the Mercurian will become extremely dangerous, for he grows secretive, which Mercury is not by nature. Then all these talents for mischief may lead him to crime, such as forgery, perjury, even poisoning.

The defect against which all those born under Mercury ought to guard themselves with a tireless vigilance is a temptation to lie and an irresistible inclination to annex too freely other people's property by schemes that are called "clever business devices" by the unscrupulous. Then again, they talk too much for the sake of boasting of their various feats of cleverness, and this weakness leads them into all manner of trouble.

6. THE SUN

The Solarians—or those born under the influence of the Sun—are of an average size, handsome and well built; their complexion has a sort of golden tint; their hair is often a beautiful blond color, wavy and abundant; their forehead is well developed but too high; it denotes at once the uncommonly brainy type of the subject. The eyes are large, of a graceful shape, full of fire and yet gentle in expression; they are somewhat prominent and the eyesight is easily affected. The face is well rounded, the mouth is arched and the teeth regular but somewhat yellowish in tint; the chin is round and firm. The body is admirably shaped, the bearing is proud and stately, but in the good Solarian there is no trace of silly vanity. They are, intellectually, a very superior race and no other star endows its subjects with such a taste for all the arts. They are dreamers of beautiful dreams and although not what one calls "practical," they are singularly successful. Often it seems as if everything they touched turned into gold. They are essentially lucky and their gambling or speculating ventures seldom fail to ultimately enrich them, especially if they obey their own inspirations. Their great

defects are: a great deal of unconscious
selfishness, and, as a natural result, a lack
of constancy in their affections. Thus
these most amiable and charming indi-
viduals render the people devoted to them
very unhappy and discouraged.

The Solarians are often called to the
highest positions in the world they belong
to, as their flowery eloquence and charming
personality dazzle their listeners. They are
not shrewd in business matters and, being
accessible to flattery, are frequently the vic-
tims of sharpers and adventurers. In brief,
they are the spoiled children of Nature and
if they realize their weak points in good
time, they have a magnificent existence
before them.

7. THE MOON

You have doubtless noticed by this time
that words in every-day use, such as "jovial,"
"saturnian," "mercurial," "sunny," applied
to the dispositions of the human temper correspond with remarkable exactitude to the
names given by Astrology to the various
planetary types. The rule holds good with
the Moon subjects, whom we call "Lunarians" (not "lunatics").

These Lunarians are above the average

height, with blond hair, rather prominent, light-colored eyes and a round head with somewhat bulging brow. They are stout, but this is often due to an ultra-lymphatic temperament. They have a tendency to dropsy and kidney diseases. The hair falls easily and so do the teeth; there is a sort of vague expression in the eyes, which are often watery. To the Lunarian type belong the nervous, hysterical temperaments, easily hypnotized and genuinely clairvoyant. Their intuition is all the more remarkable, since they are very poor reasoners and are swayed to and fro by an ever-working imagination. Their nature is seldom well-balanced and, unless properly trained or protected by "friendly" Planets in favorable aspects, the Lunarians may end in insane asylums as "lunatics."

However, a fair amount of Moon influence may be beneficial, especially to those whose profession calls for a constant supply of imagination, such as poets, novelists, composers, and even painters and sculptors. As a rule it is among women that one finds the greatest number of Lunarians; their special physical troubles are also very powerfully influenced by the Moon. Intuition, this precious gift of the weaker sex, is due to the same planet; finally, the Lunarians are decidedly hypochondriac, that is, constantly imagining themselves the prey of some disease or other.

This closes my present review of the Planets' characteristics. Remember, this is only the ground-work of what is coming later; but, like every other kind of ground-work, it is an essential part of the structure and has to be studied in all its details, if any satisfactory results are to be secured.

SYMBOLS OF THE PLANETS AND ZODIACAL SIGNS

Saturn	♄	Aries	♈	Libra	♎
Jupiter	♃	Taurus	♉	Scorpio	♏
Mars	♂	Gemini	♊	Sagittarius	♐
Sun	☉	Cancer	♋	Capricorn	♑
Venus	♀	Leo	♌	Aquarius	♒
Mercury	☿	Virgo	♍	Pisces	♓
Moon	☽				

CHAPTER V

THE TWELVE SOLAR HOUSES

We have studied, sufficiently for all prac·
tical purposes, the first two elements of a
Horoscope, namely, "the 12 signs of the
Zodiac" and "the 6 Planets." Now we
reach the third element, which, intelligently
combined with the two others, will give us
the most extraordinary inside view into the
lives of the subjects under inspection.

This new and distinct element in our
study consists in another method of dividing
the Zodiac, discovered or prescribed by the
ancient Magi, and their successors, the
Egyptian Priests. Here again, the Zodiac
is divided into twelve equal parts, called this
time "Solar Houses," and designated by the
numerals I. to XII. in Roman figures.

The student will remember that, when we
began our examination of the Signs of the
Zodiac, we placed the first Sign, "Aries," in
what is called the "Orient" (= East) of the
Zodiacal circle. This same space (to the
left hand of the reader when examining a

diagram of the Zodiac) is permanently occupied by House I. Proceeding downward to
what is called the "Bottom" of the Horos-

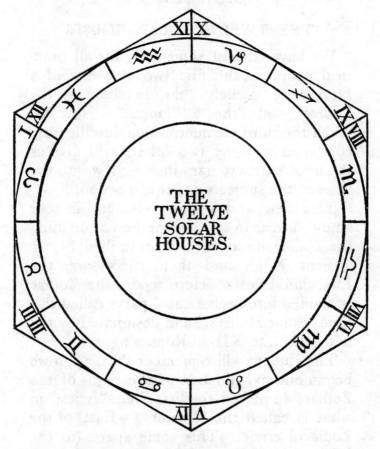

THE
TWELVE
SOLAR
HOUSES.

cupe, we place House II. in the compartment
reserved for "Taurus."

Continuing in the same direction we place:

House   III. in "Gemini."
House   IV. in "Cancer."
House   V. in "Leo."
House   VI. in "Virgo."
House   VII. in "Libra."
House VIII. in "Scorpio."
House   IX. in "Sagittarius."
House   X. in "Capricorn."
House   XI. in "Aquarius."
House   XII. in "Pisces."

The illustration in this Chapter locates the 12 Houses in accordance with the above enumeration. Now, this is the position of the Houses in every Horoscope; *they never change.*

On the other hand, the Signs of the Zodiac, although keeping in their immutable order, are "oriented" (placed) in such a manner that the sign containing the date of the subject's birth always occupies the space which is devoted to Aries when the Zodiac is, as above, examined by itself and without having any particular individual in view. In other words, the sign representing the date of birth is invariably placed in House I.

As an example, let us suppose that the

subject was born on September 23, i. e., in the second degree of Libra. After drawing a circle and dividing it into twelve equal parts, we shall place the sign of Libra where, in our illustration, Aries is marked. Then, working our way downward, we will place:

> Scorpio where Taurus was.
> Sagittarius where Gemini was.
> Capricorn where Cancer was.
> Aquarius where Leo was.
> Pisces where Virgo was.
> Aries where Libra was.
> Taurus where Scorpio was.
> Gemini where Sagittarius was.
> Cancer where Capricorn was.
> Leo where Aquarius was.
> Virgo where Pisces was.

In such a Horoscope the signs are located in the following Houses:

Libra in House I.; Scorpio in House II.; Sagittarius in House III.; Capricorn in House IV.; Aquarius in House V.; Pisces in House VI.; Aries in House VII.; Taurus in House VIII.; Gemini in House IX.; Cancer in House X.; Leo in House XI.; Virgo in House XII.

As each of the Houses embraces one or more of the leading features of man or woman's physical, mental, and moral characteristics, as well as all the important events of his or her life, the clear understanding of the meanings of the Solar Houses—not only by themselves but in connection with the signs of the Zodiac which the fatality of birth has caused to be located in each of the Houses—brings us a wide step nearer to a complete comprehension of the Astrological mysteries.

Let me give you first the grouping of the twelve Houses in four divisions of high philosophical importance and at the same time of real practical utility for every student. And in this connection, allow me to remind you of the divisions of the Signs of the Zodiac into the four Trinocracies: *Fire, Earth, Air* and *Water.*

Here we have also four groups:

First Group: House I., V., IX.—These represent the life of the subject:—House I., his own life and type. House V., his life in his children. House IX., his life in the upper world, in God; his religion.

Second Group: Houses X., VI., II.—These represent the activity, honors and money-making possibilities of the subject.—House X., refers to what is not financial, in one's prosperity, such as promotions, honors, etc.,

House VI., to the possessions of the subject that are of an animated nature, such as slaves, cattle, etc. House II., treats of the other kinds of wealth.

Third Group: Houses VII., III., XI.— They represent love in its various manifestations.—House VII., refers to marriage, and in general to love between the sexes. House III., to blood relations. House XI., to friends.

Fourth Group: Houses IV., XII., VIII.— They represent old age, illness and death.— House IV., refers to the various traits that come by heredity. House XII., to all the troubles that may affect us: disease, imprisonment, exile, etc. House VIII., reveals the time and manner of death.

Almost as a matter of course, its next neighbor, House IX., is devoted to such revelations as refer to the Supreme Being and a future life.

In these elementary lessons I try to avoid, as much as possible, the introduction of too many technical words, and yet I must speak here of two other divisions of the Houses, which are referred to frequently in more extended Astrological works. The first is as follows:

Houses I., IV., VII. and X. are called "Cardinal" or "Angular."

Houses II., V., VIII. and XI. are called "Succedent."

Houses III. VI., IX. and XII are called "Cadent."

The second division is as follows:

Good or "Favorable": Houses I., II., V., VII., X.

Indifferent or "Middling": Houses III., IV., IX., XI.

Bad or "Unfavorable": Houses VI., VIII., XII.

I wish I had the space and time to demonstrate to you that the apparent disorder in the arrangement of the Houses is, in reality, a most admirable and logical grouping of all the elements that compose a human existence. I will only add this—which applies to everything I have taught you so far: no single department of Astrological study—either the characteristics of the Signs of Zodiac, or the nature and position of the Planets, or the location and meanings of the Solar Houses, taken separately and apart from the other elements of study, could suffice to cast a reliable Horoscope, although in many respects it may furnish surprisingly accurate data. It is

4

only the combined examination of all these three great components that brings forth a true and worthy Horoscope. We are studying now each of these elements separately, but in a short time I shall be able to initiate you a little further, and to place in your hands the key of one of the most curious and trustworthy of the occult sciences.

As stated above, we find in each House accurate information referring to some special characteristics or events concerning the person under examination.

HOUSE I.

Thus, House I., called also "the Horoscope" or "the House of Nativity," is especially rich in details concerning the subject's type, his physical, mental and moral propensities, and his past, present and future health. Here, also, we find everything concerning the duration of life and possible accidents, especially those that might affect the head.

HOUSE II.

House II. furnishes information about pecuniary transactions, their success or failure, the probabilities of becoming rich at

some time or other, whether it be advisable
to take risks in money matters or, on the
contrary, to be satisfied with a moderate
competence acquired without resorting to
any speculative ventures.   It also tells gamblers when, and when not, to tempt fickle
fortune.

A close study of all the various features of astrology proves a fairly sure
guide in all enterprises that possess an element of danger.   But a long experience is
necessary before such revelations are to be
trusted at all.   Beware of so-called astrologers who offer their services to speculators
on the Board of Trade or the Stock Ex-
change; as a rule, they are absolute frauds,
as they do not give themselves the trouble
to go deep enough in the arcana of our science to obtain reliable answers to their
clients' queries.   In most cases they are not
astrologers at all, but simply swindlers.

HOUSE III.

House III. will tell you everything of
interest concerning your brothers, sisters,
and other collateral relatives.   It reveals
also when travels and minor changes in the
subject's existence are to take place, also
the influence of passing acquaintances.

HOUSE IV.

House IV. refers to parents and ancestors in the direct line; to inheritances, legacies, family secrets, mysteries of all kinds in which the subject, his parents and his direct descendants are interested. A loss of position due to some family stain or disaster is also occasionally found marked in this House.

HOUSE V.

House V. is known as the "House of Good Fortune," and in it most of the joys of life are discovered. Our love affairs, either ending in marriage or otherwise; our children; success in our career, the satisfactions of our pride; the presents we receive, and the rewards that come to us—deserved or not—all these and many others of similar nature are predicted to us by astrological readings based on the occupants of House V.

HOUSE VI.

House VI. used to be dubbed, by the ancient astrologers, the "Hospital of the Zodiac," and it truly deserves this appellation, since it is there that we are notified of everything concerning our illnesses, our most serious disappointments, the cruel blows that Fate has in reserve for us, and our repeated failure to triumph over "what has been written." In the same House we must look for all that concerns our inferiors, our servants, our dependents.

HOUSE VII.

House VII. is the revealer of such things as relate to marriage and every kind of partnership. Strange to say, it is here also that we are apprized of our open enemies' attacks, of fights, and—should we be rulers of our fellow-beings—of the wars we shall have to wage or which will be waged against us. The fact that this House is directly opposite to House I., the House of the subject's birth—renders it dangerous and inimical to the very existence of the person under examination. Separations, divorces, grave disagreements in matters of affection and interest are also found predicted herein.

HOUSE VIII.

House VIII. divides with Houses VI. and XII. the worst prognostics that are furnished by astrological examinations. It tells of sorrows, of the loss of beloved ones, of serious wounds, of fatal accidents, of diseases, and of death. The only consolation we can sometimes extract from this

House is the announcement of unexpected inheritances, of gifts of importance coming to us unexpected, but welcome.

HOUSE IX.

House IX. reminds us of the resources and holy balm to be found in religion, of the possible development of our higher brain-power, of our abilities for philosophical studies, of our love for delving into the mysterious realms of the occult. Whenever this House is well endowed with Signs and Stars in their favorable aspects, you may feel certain that the subject is a person of very unusual accomplishments.

HOUSE X.

House X. is the revealing center of all the honors and dignities that may gild the life-horizon of the person under examination. Remember that it does not promise the realization of foolish ambitions, entirely out of porportion to the subject's position in life. But, within the sphere where Fate has placed his lot, he will be looked up to as a leader, and if he is never to be "the second in Rome," he is fairly sure to be "first in his village." In one's calling or profession, prominence is in the gift of this House; it is

believed by many astrologers that House
X. gives more vain glory than moneyed success.   As a side issue, we often consult
House X. for information on the subject's
mother, while in House IV. the father's fate
is found predicted or related.

HOUSE XI.

House XI. is the revealer of the benefac-
tors and the true friends it may be our lot to
meet during life.   They are, as we all know
to our sorrow, few and far between, and so
are the disinterested protectors also an-
nounced in this House.   Finally, by the fact
of its being exactly opposite House V. we
obtain here supplementary information concerning our children, the alliances (matrimonial or other) we may contract, and we
are also told sometimes of the chances of
seeing our most cherished hopes realized.

HOUSE XII.

House XII. is undoubtedly the worst of
the 12 Zoadical habitations, especially for
those who do not consider death as being
the greatest evil man is heir to.   It refers to
the troubles and heart burnings coming to
us from the treachery of friends; to cease-
less persecutions rendering our life more

than a purgatory; to calumny pursuing us relentlessly, to imprisonment, exile, wretched poverty, unutterable discouragement and despair.

And this ends my rapid examination of the 12 Houses, the close study of which I take the liberty of particularly recommending to my readers.

CHAPTER VI

THE THIRTY-SIX DECANS

Now that we have obtained a pretty fair and accurate idea of the three main elements of Astrological lore, to-wit: The Signs of the Zodiac, the Planets and the Solar Houses, I want to enter into some further revelations which you will not find in any other works of the kind published on this side of the water or in England. I refer to the meanings given to the divisions of the 12 Signs of the Zodiac.

You must be told first, that the Egyptian priests—who became the depositories and perfectors of the ancient science of predicting man's fate from the stars—had placed each Zoadical period of 30 days under the guardianship of one of the supernatural beings we call "genii." They further divided each sign into periods of 10 days, assuming some particular spirit as the power dominating over each of these spaces of 10 days. Finally, each day had its demi-god in charge and its separate interpretation.

I do not intend to give you here the names of these strange and powerful beings nor do I propose to explain the meanings and prognostics attached to every one of the 365 days of the year. But, to come a little closer to the understanding of the nature of the subject under examination, I will insert in this volume of brief lessons, the positive and most reliable statements that concern each one of these periods of ten days called in Astrological parlance "Decans" from the Greek word "deka," meaning "ten." Instead of following the usual order of the Signs and beginning the year in March, I will start from January 1st.

JANUARY

Decan 1. From January 1 to 10 (Capricorn, 12 to 21).—Intelligence devoted to useless pursuit. Constant scheming of unpractical affairs. Warlike disposition.

Decan II. January 11 to 20 (Capricorn, 22 to Aquarius 1).—Suspicious, skeptical mind; impotence, timidity.

Decan III. January 21 to 30 (Aquarius, 2 to 11).—Anxiety due to hard struggle for life. Disappointed ambition. Delay in the realization in one's hopes. Illness in infancy due to neglect of the nurse.

FEBRUARY

Decan I. January 31 to February 9 (Aquarius, 12 to 21).—Well endowed brain-power. Gentleness of temper, private virtues.

Decan II. February 10 to 19 (Aquarius 22 to Pisces 1).—Extremely delicate childhood until 7 years old. Persistent difficulties through life. Bitter disappointments.

Decan III. February 20 to 28 (Pisces 2 to 10).—Great ambitions, love of glory; boldness in everything the subject undertakes.

MARCH

Decan I. March 1 to 10 (Pisces, 11 to 20). —Indolence, love of pleasure, sluggish mind.

Decan II. March 11 to 20 (Pisces, 21 to 30).—Restless disposition, confused scheming, fickle tendencies, yearnings for impossible things.

Decan III. March 21 to 30 (Aries, 1 to 10).—Firm, haughty disposition. Contempt for all obstacles and perils.

APRIL

Decan I. March 31 to April 9 (Aries, 11 to 20). Noble nature, generosity, aptitude for commanding, diplomatic talent.

Decan II. April 10 to 19 (Aries, 21 to 30).
Quick and versatile mind. Love of pleasure.

Decan III. April 20 to 29 (Taurus 1 to 10).
—High intellectual faculties, inclination
toward the exact sciences and political
economy. The subject will meet with
serious reverses, some of these of a violent
character.

MAY

Decan I. April 30 to May 9 (Taurus, 11 to
20).—Generosity of mind and heart, lofty
inclinations, distinctions due to merit; eloquence.

Decan II. May 10 to 19 (Taurus, 21 to 30).
—Obstacles to enterprises; obligation to
submit to the authority of others in spite of
a naturally independent temper; troubles
against which the subject must fight with all
possible energy.

Decan III. May 20 to 29 (Gemini, 1 to
19).—Restless disposition which will destroy
the subject's chances in life. Threat of
violent death.

JUNE

Decan I. May 30 to June 8 (Gemini, 11 to
20).—Careless, thoughtless disposition;
superficiality, poor understanding of own
best interest. Useless, often senseless, talk.

Decan II. June 9 to 18 (Gemini, 21 to 30).
—Inclination toward the purely theoretical
branches of knowledge that bring neither
profit nor glory. Troubles through life.
Serious disaster early in life.

Decan III. June 19 to July 3.—This period
includes the five Epagomenes or Supplementary Days, thus completing the full 365
days of our regular year. (Cancer, 1 to 10).
—Bright, quick mind, sociable instincts.

JULY

Decan I. July 4 to 13 (Cancer, 11 to 20).—
Abrupt manners. Love of the arts and
sciences. Great luck in money-making.

Decan II. July 14 to 23 (Cancer, 21 to 30).
—Hard, inflexible temperament, calling
upon force to carry out its wishes. Sea-
voyages predicted.

Decan III. July 24 to August 2 (Leo, 1 to
19).—Violent disposition, fiery passions,
often celebrity acquired in such arts as
sculpture, architecture, engineering, etc., or
as a playwright.

AUGUST

Decan I. August 3 to 12 (Leo, 11 to 20).—
Phlegmatic temperament; force of inertia,
exaggerated self-confidence. Talent for the
plastic arts. Conceit.

Decan II. August 13 to 22 (Leo, 21 to 30).
—Great persistency of purpose, egotism,
adventurous disposition, highly successful
ambition through luck and thanks to a combative spirit.   Several marriages.

Decan III. August 23 to September 1
(Virgo, 1 to 10).—Longevity; timidity; aptitude for the analytical sciences and the
mechanical arts.

SEPTEMBER

Decan I. September 2 to 11 (Virgo, 11 to
20).—Orderly and saving disposition, sometimes to the point of penuriousness. Patient
perseverance in all undertakings.

Decan II. September 12 to 21 (Virgo, 21
to 30).—A passion for gambling or other
forms of speculative ventures. Incapacity
for useful productiveness, destructive tendencies. Grave fatalities on account of an
unfortunate marriage or through relatives.
Often an inventive genius.

Decan III. September 22 to October 1
(Libra, 1 to 10).—Love of justice and of
truth; feeling of what is right; impulse to
defend the weak against all oppression.

OCTOBER

Decan I. October 2 to 11 (Libra, 11 to 20).
—Ambitious and restless mind.   Great

cleverness in the handling of men; audacity; success in all bold enterprises.

Decan II. October 12 to 21 (Libra, 21 to 30).—Intense love of all kinds of pleasures, of luxury and of the society of the other sex.

Decan III. October 22 to 31 (Scorpio, 1 to 10).—Disappointment, treachery often met with, perilous travels, chimerical enterprises.

NOVEMBER

Decan I. November 1 to 10 (Scorpio, 11 to 20).—Enmity from influential people that will threaten to ruin even the best prospects.

Decan II. November 11 to 20 (Scorpio, 21 to 30).—Ardent passions, unbending disposition, energy that knows no defeat.

Decan III. November 21 to 30 (Sagittarius, 1 to 10).—Haughty disposition, extreme love of independence. Brilliant military career; disastrous married life.

DECEMBER

Decan I. December 1 to 10 (Sagittarius, 11 to 20).—Deeply religious turn of mind. Great struggles all through life, terrible fits of anger. Gloomy temper. Scientifically inclined. Many unforeseen perils. Frankness mixed with a great mobility of impressions.

Decan II. December 11 to 20 (Sagittarius, 21 to 30). — Obstinacy, violent temper, shrewdness, often dishonest, versatility, fighting instincts.

Decan III. December 21 to 31 (Capricorn, 1 to 11).—Disastrous journeys, alternatives of very good and very bad fortune, great love sorrows.

Completing the above statements concerning the Decans the reader must know, that, just as each Sign of the Zodiac is the seat of the Thrones (diurnal or nocturnal) of one of the seven Planets, just so one of these Planets is in charge of each of the Decans, except when the astrological calculations place it somewhere else. I will give herein the list of these "Influences of the Decans."

ARIES

DECAN I. Mars. DECAN II. The Sun. DECAN III. Venus.

TAURUS

DECAN I. Mercury. DECAN II. The Moon. DECAN III. Saturn.

GEMINI

DECAN I. Jupiter. DECAN II. Mars. DE-
CAN III. The Sun.

CANCER

DECAN I. Venus. DECAN II. Mercury. DE-
CAN III. The Moon.

LEO

DECAN I. Saturn. DECAN II. Jupiter. DE-
CAN III. Mars.

VIRGO

DECAN I. The Sun. DECAN II. Venus. DE-
CAN III. Mercury.

LIBRA

DECAN I. The Moon. DECAN II. Saturn.
DECAN III. Jupiter.

SCORPIO

DECAN I. Mars. DECAN II. The Sun. DE-
CAN III. Venus.

SAGITTARIUS

DECAN I. Mercury. DECAN II. The Moon.
DECAN III. Saturn.

CAPRICORN

DECAN I. Jupiter. DECAN II. Mars. DE-
CAN III. The Sun.

AQUARIUS

DECAN I. Venus. DECAN II. Mercury. DE-
CAN III. The Moon.

PISCES

DECAN I. Saturn. DECAN II. Jupiter. DE-
CAN III. Mars.

Now let me tell you how the knowledge of the influence of the planets on the Decans may be used by you to advantage.

After you have located a birthday where it belongs, in one of the degrees of one of the signs of the Zodiac, you must read carefully the various characteristics I gave you in Chapter III. as referring to those born under this, or that, particular sign. Then, turning to Chapter IV. you will read what I have taught you concerning the various planetary types. If the subject you are studying—either yourself or anyone else, even a total stranger—is born, say on August 3d, i. e., in the 9th degree of Leo, which belongs, of course, to the first Decan of the said Sign, you will find, by referring to the above table, that your subject was directly influenced at birth by the planet Saturn. Thus the reading of what I have told you about Leo and Saturn will already give you a much deeper insight into this particular person's real nature and into his, or her, past or future, than could be obtained simply by Zodiacal data. But this is anticipating a little, as I reserve for our future lessons the systematic working out of all the mass of classified information herein contained.

CHAPTER VII

THE ZODIACAL CALENDAR

Day	Sign	Degree	Day	Sign	Degree
Jan. 1	Capricorn	12	Feb. 1	Aquarius	13
Jan. 2	Capricorn	13	Feb. 2	Aquarius	14
Jan. 3	Capricorn	14	Feb. 3	Aquarius	15
Jan. 4	Capricorn	15	Feb. 4	Aquarius	16
Jan. 5	Capricorn	16	Feb. 5	Aquarius	17
Jan. 6	Capricorn	17	Feb. 6	Aquarius	18
Jan. 7	Capricorn	18	Feb. 7	Aquarius	19
Jan. 8	Capricorn	19	Feb. 8	Aquarius	20
Jan. 9	Capricorn	20	Feb. 9	Aquarius	21
Jan. 10	Capricorn	21	Feb. 10	Aquarius	22
Jan. 11	Capricorn	22	Feb. 11	Aquarius	23
Jan. 12	Capricorn	23	Feb. 12	Aquarius	24
Jan. 13	Capricorn	24	Feb. 13	Aquarius	25
Jan. 14	Capricorn	25	Feb. 14	Aquarius	26
Jan. 15	Capricorn	26	Feb. 15	Aquarius	27
Jan. 16	Capricorn	27	Feb. 16	Aquarius	28
Jan. 17	Capricorn	28	Feb. 17	Aquarius	29
Jan. 18	Capricorn	29	Feb. 18	Aquarius	30
Jan. 19	Capricorn	30			
			Feb. 19	Pisces	1
Jan. 20	Aquarius	1	Feb. 20	Pisces	2
Jan. 21	Aquarius	2	Feb. 21	Pisces	3
Jan. 22	Aquarius	3	Feb. 22	Pisces	4
Jan. 23	Aquarius	4	Feb. 23	Pisces	5
Jan. 24	Aquarius	5	Feb. 24	Pisces	6
Jan. 25	Aquarius	6	Feb. 25	Pisces	7
Jan. 26	Aquarius	7	Feb. 26	Pisces	8
Jan. 27	Aquarius	8	Feb. 27	Pisces	9
Jan. 28	Aquarius	9	Feb. 28	Pisces	10
Jan. 29	Aquarius	10	Feb. 29	Pisces	11
Jan. 30	Aquarius	11			
Jan. 31	Aquarius	12			

THE ZODIACAL CALENDAR

(CONTINUED)

Day	Sign	Degree	Day	Sign	Degree
Mar. 1	Pisces	11	Apr. 1	Aries	12
Mar. 2	Pisces	12	Apr. 2	Aries	13
Mar. 3	Pisces	13	Apr. 3	Aries	14
Mar. 4	Pisces	14	Apr. 4	Aries	15
Mar. 5	Pisces	15	Apr. 5	Aries	16
Mar. 6	Pisces	16	Apr. 6	Aries	17
Mar. 7	Pisces	17	Apr. 7	Aries	18
Mar. 8	Pisces	18	Apr. 8	Aries	19
Mar. 9	Pisces	19	Apr. 9	Aries	20
Mar. 10	Pisces	20	Apr. 10	Aries	21
Mar. 11	Pisces	21	Apr. 11	Aries	22
Mar. 12	Pisces	22	Apr. 12	Aries	23
Mar. 13	Pisces	23	Apr. 13	Aries	24
Mar. 14	Pisces	24	Apr. 14	Aries	25
Mar. 15	Pisces	25	Apr. 15	Aries	26
Mar. 16	Pisces	26	Apr. 16	Aries	27
Mar. 17	Pisces	27	Apr. 17	Aries	28
Mar. 18	Pisces	28	Apr. 18	Aries	29
Mar. 19	Pisces	29	Apr. 19	Aries	30
Mar. 20	Pisces	30			
			Apr. 20	Taurus	1
Mar. 21	Aries	1	Apr. 21	Taurus	2
Mar. 22	Aries	2	Apr. 22	Taurus	3
Mar. 23	Aries	3	Apr. 23	Taurus	4
Mar. 24	Aries	4	Apr. 24	Taurus	5
Mar. 25	Aries	5	Apr. 25	Taurus	6
Mar. 26	Aries	6	Apr. 26	Taurus	7
Mar. 27	Aries	7	Apr. 27	Taurus	8
Mar. 28	Aries	8	Apr. 28	Taurus	9
Mar. 29	Aries	9	Apr. 29	Taurus	10
Mar. 30	Aries	10	Apr. 30	Taurus	11
Mar 31	Aries	11			

(CONTINUED)

Day	Sign	Degree	Day	Sign	Degree
May 1	Taurus	12	June 1	Gemini	13
May 2	Taurus	13	June 2	Gemini	14
May 3	Taurus	14	June 3	Gemini	15
May 4	Taurus	15	June 4	Gemini	16
May 5	Taurus	16	June 5	Gemini	17
May 6	Taurus	17	June 6	Gemini	18
May 7	Taurus	18	June 7	Gemini	19
May 8	Taurus	19	June 8	Gemini	20
May 9	Taurus	20	June 9	Gemini	21
May 10	Taurus	21	June 10	Gemini	22
May 11	Taurus	22	June 11	Gemini	23
May 12	Taurus	23	June 12	Gemini	24
May 13	Taurus	24	June 13	Gemini	25
May 14	Taurus	25	June 14	Gemini	26
May 15	Taurus	26	June 15	Gemini	27
May 16	Taurus	27	June 16	Gemini	28
May 17	Taurus	28	June 17	Gemini	29
May 18	Taurus	29	June 18	Gemini	30
May 19	Taurus	30			
			June 19	Cancer	} 1
May 20	Gemini	1	June 20	Epagomene	
May 21	Gemini	2	June 21	Cancer	} 2
May 22	Gemini	3	June 22	Epagomene	
May 23	Gemini	4	June 23	Cancer	} 3
May 24	Gemini	5	June 24	Epagomene	
May 25	Gemini	6	June 25	Cancer	} 4
May 26	Gemini	7	June 26	Epagomene	
May 27	Gemini	8	June 27	Cancer	} 5
May 28	Gemini	9	June 28	Epagomene	
May 29	Gemini	10	June 29	Cancer	6
May 30	Gemini	11	June 30	Cancer	7
May 31	Gemini	12			

THE ZODIACAL CALENDAR

(Continued)

Day	Sign	Degree	Day	Sign	Degree
July 1	Cancer	8	Aug. 1	Leo	9
July 2	Cancer	9	Aug. 2	Leo	10
July 3	Cancer	10	Aug. 3	Leo	11
July 4	Cancer	11	Aug. 4	Leo	12
July 5	Cancer	12	Aug. 5	Leo	13
July 6	Cancer	13	Aug. 6	Leo	14
July 7	Cancer	14	Aug. 7	Leo	15
July 8	Cancer	15	Aug. 8	Leo	16
July 9	Cancer	16	Aug. 9	Leo	17
July 10	Cancer	17	Aug. 10	Leo	18
July 11	Cancer	18	Aug. 11	Leo	19
July 12	Cancer	19	Aug. 12	Leo	20
July 13	Cancer	20	Aug. 13	Leo	21
July 14	Cancer	21	Aug. 14	Leo	22
July 15	Cancer	22	Aug. 15	Leo	23
July 16	Cancer	23	Aug. 16	Leo	24
July 17	Cancer	24	Aug. 17	Leo	25
July 18	Cancer	25	Aug. 18	Leo	26
July 19	Cancer	26	Aug. 19	Leo	27
July 20	Cancer	27	Aug. 20	Leo	28
July 21	Cancer	28	Aug. 21	Leo	29
July 22	Cancer	29	Aug. 22	Leo	30
July 23	Cancer	30			
			Aug. 23	Virgo	1
July 24	Leo	1	Aug. 24	Virgo	2
July 25	Leo	2	Aug. 25	Virgo	3
July 26	Leo	3	Aug. 26	Virgo	4
July 27	Leo	4	Aug. 27	Virgo	5
July 28	Leo	5	Aug. 28	Virgo	6
July 29	Leo	6	Aug. 29	Virgo	7
July 30	Leo	7	Aug. 30	Virgo	8
July 31	Leo	8	Aug. 31	Virgo	9

(Continued)

Day	Sign	Degree	Day	Sign	Degree
Sept. 1	Virgo	10	Oct. 1	Libra	10
Sept. 2	Virgo	11	Oct. 2	Libra	11
Sept. 3	Virgo	12	Oct. 3	Libra	12
Sept. 4	Virgo	13	Oct. 4	Libra	13
Sept. 5	Virgo	14	Oct. 5	Libra	14
Sept. 6	Virgo	15	Oct. 6	Libra	15
Sept. 7	Virgo	16	Oct. 7	Libra	16
Sept. 8	Virgo	17	Oct. 8	Libra	17
Sept. 9	Virgo	18	Oct. 9	Libra	18
Sept. 10	Virgo	19	Oct. 10	Libra	19
Sept. 11	Virgo	20	Oct. 11	Libra	20
Sept. 12	Virgo	21	Oct. 12	Libra	21
Sept. 13	Virgo	22	Oct. 13	Libra	22
Sept. 14	Virgo	23	Oct. 14	Libra	23
Sept. 15	Virgo	24	Oct. 15	Libra	24
Sept. 16	Virgo	25	Oct. 16	Libra	25
Sept. 17	Virgo	26	Oct. 17	Libra	26
Sept. 18	Virgo	27	Oct. 18	Libra	27
Sept. 19	Virgo	28	Oct. 19	Libra	28
Sept. 20	Virgo	29	Oct. 20	Libra	29
Sept. 21	Virgo	30	Oct. 21	Libra	30
Sept. 22	Libra	1	Oct. 22	Scorpio	1
Sept. 23	Libra	2	Oct. 23	Scorpio	2
Sept. 24	Libra	3	Oct. 24	Scorpio	3
Sept. 25	Libra	4	Oct. 25	Scorpio	4
Sept. 26	Libra	5	Oct. 26	Scorpio	5
Sept. 27	Libra	6	Oct. 27	Scorpio	6
Sept. 28	Libra	7	Oct. 28	Scorpio	7
Sept. 29	Libra	8	Oct. 29	Scorpio	8
Sept. 30	Libra	9	Oct. 30	Scorpio	9
			Oct. 31	Scorpio	10

THE ZODIACAL CALENDAR

(Continued)

Day	Sign	Degree	Day	Sign	Degree
Nov. 1	Scorpio	11	Dec. 1	Sagittarius	11
Nov. 2	Scorpio	12	Dec. 2	Sagittarius	12
Nov. 3	Scorpio	13	Dec. 3	Sagittarius	13
Nov. 4	Scorpio	14	Dec. 4	Sagittarius	14
Nov. 5	Scorpio	15	Dec. 5	Sagittarius	15
Nov. 6	Scorpio	16	Dec. 6	Sagittarius	16
Nov. 7	Scorpio	17	Dec. 7	Sagittarius	17
Nov. 8	Scorpio	18	Dec. 8	Sagittarius	18
Nov. 9	Scorpio	19	Dec. 9	Sagittarius	19
Nov. 10	Scorpio	20	Dec. 10	Sagittarius	20
Nov. 11	Scorpio	21	Dec. 11	Sagittarius	21
Nov. 12	Scorpio	22	Dec. 12	Sagittarius	22
Nov. 13	Scorpio	23	Dec. 13	Sagittarius	25
Nov. 14	Scorpio	24	Dec. 14	Sagittarius	24
Nov. 15	Scorpio	25	Dec. 15	Sagittarius	25
Nov. 16	Scorpio	26	Dec. 16	Sagittarius	26
Nov. 17	Scorpio	27	Dec. 17	Sagittarius	27
Nov. 18	Scorpio	28	Dec. 18	Sagittarius	28
Nov. 19	Scorpio	29	Dec. 19	Sagittarius	29
Nov. 20	Scorpio	30	Dec. 20	Sagittarius	30
Nov. 21	Sagittarius	1	Dec. 21	Capricorn	1
Nov. 22	Sagittarius	2	Dec. 22	Capricorn	2
Nov. 23	Sagittarius	3	Dec. 23	Capricorn	3
Nov. 24	Sagittarius	4	Dec. 24	Capricorn	4
Nov. 25	Sagittarius	5	Dec. 25	Capricorn	5
Nov. 26	Sagittarius	6	Dec. 26	Capricorn	6
Nov. 27	Sagittarius	7	Dec. 27	Capricorn	7
Nov. 28	Sagittarius	8	Dec. 28	Capricorn	8
Nov. 29	Sagittarius	9	Dec. 29	Capricorn	9
Nov. 30	Sagittarius	10	Dec. 30	Capricorn	10
			Dec. 31	Capricorn	11

CHAPTER VIII

THE ASPECTS

The special object of this chapter is the explanation of what is meant by "Astrological Aspects," and the practical use to which the knowledge of these Aspects can be put for the proper casting of a Horoscope.

Will you kindly look back to my illustration, page 80, entitled "The Planets on their Thrones"? We will suppose for a moment, that in somebody's Horoscope these luminaries are all occupying both their Thrones at the same moment. Now you will admit that, around the Zodiacal circle, these planets seem to be gazing at each other, so to speak, at different angles. Thus, if we take Saturn in Capricorn as the starting point (as I do in my illustration, page 124), Saturn is said to be

in SEMI-SEXTILE ASPECT ($\frac{1}{12}$) toward Jupiter in Sagittarius.

in SEXTILE ASPECT ($\frac{1}{6}$) toward Mars in Scorpio.

in SQUARE ASPECT ($\frac{1}{4}$) toward Venus in Libra.

in TRINE ASPECT (⅓) toward Mercury in
Virgo.
in SESQUIQUADRATE ASPECT ($\frac{5}{12}$) toward the
Sun in Leo.
in OPPOSITION ASPECT (½) toward the Moon
in Cancer.

In the accompanying illustration, I give
the symbols or marks by which these six
different aspects are indicated for short.

The seventh aspect is called *conjunction* and takes place whenever two or more planets are found in the same Zodiacal sign. Now keep in mind the two following statements:

First. By "Aspects" is always meant the positions of the PLANETS respecting each other, as these vary constantly. The positions of the Signs of the Zodiac in respect to each other is immutable and cannot be referred to by the term "aspect."

Second. By my system, which is nothing more or less than the exact restoration of the oldest conception of the influence of the heavenly bodies upon the types and destinies of mankind, it constantly happens that the same planet appears several times in the same Horoscope of birth. Thus an almost infinite number of combinations of Aspects is formed; but numerous as they are, they are easily grouped together, so that even a very indifferent student may grasp their leading meanings.

I gave you the names and positions of the seven Aspects, but I do not advise you to use, nor do I use myself, more than five of these "points of view." These are: CONJUNCTION, SEXTILE, SQUARE, TRINE, and

OPPOSITION. The Rule in reference to Aspects is simply and invariably this:

1. Planets separated by *one* full Sign, or 60 degrees, are in SEXTILE ASPECT.

2. Planets separated by *two* full Signs, or 90 degrees, are in SQUARE ASPECT.

3. Planets separated by *three* full Signs, or 120 degrees, are in TRINE ASPECT.

4. Planets separated by *four* full Signs, or 180 Degrees, are in OPPOSITION ASPECT.

The Semi-sextile and Sesquiquadrate Aspects are of so little consequence, comparatively speaking, that we may omit them entirely from our consideration.

Now that the Aspects have been well defined let me give you some general points concerning their Astrological value.

"Conjunction" is considered favorable only if the Planets thus brought together are "beneficent planets."

"Sextile" is always a favorable Aspect.

"Square" is an unfavorable Aspect, except between two beneficent planets.

"Trine" is always a favorable Aspect.

The "Opposition" of two planets is always considered as most unfavorable.

CHAPTER IX

THE CYCLIC TABLES OF THE YEARS

An Astrological Cycle consists of 36 years. Each such cycle is ascribed to one of the planets, in regular rotation. This planet *presides* over the 1, 8, 15, 22, 29 and 36 years of its cycle, while the other 6 planets preside over the remaining 30 years in sequence.

The cycles follow each other in the inverted order of the week days: The Sun (Sunday), Saturn (Saturday), Venus (Friday), Jupiter (Thursday), Mercury (Wednesday), Mars (Tuesday), The Moon (Monday).

The order in which the planets succeed each other within each cycle, is as follows: Saturn, Jupiter, Mars, Sun, Venus, Mercury, Moon, Saturn, Jupiter, etc.

CYCLE OF VENUS (1801—1836)

Venus,   1801, 1808, 1815, 1822, 1829, 1836.
Mercury,   1802, 1809, 1816, 1823, 1830.
The Moon,   1803, 1810, 1817, 1824, 1831.
Saturn,   1804, 1811, 1818, 1825, 1832.
Jupiter,   1805, 1812, 1819, 1826, 1833.
Mars,   1806, 1813, 1820, 1827, 1834.
The Sun,   1807, 1814, 1821, 1828, 1835.

CYCLE OF JUPITER (1837—1872)

Jupiter,   1837, 1844, 1851, 1858, 1865, 1872.
Mars,   1838, 1845, 1852, 1859, 1866.
The Sun,   1839, 1846, 1853, 1860, 1867.
Venus,   1840, 1847, 1854, 1861, 1868.
Mercury,   1841, 1848, 1855, 1862, 1869.
The Moon, 1842, 1849, 1856, 1863, 1870.
Saturn,   1843, 1850, 1857, 1864, 1871.

CYCLE OF MERCURY (1873—1908)

Mercury,   1873, 1880, 1887, 1894, 1901, 1908
The Moon, 1874, 1881, 1888, 1895, 1902.
Saturn,   1875, 1882, 1889, 1896, 1903.
Jupiter,   1876, 1883, 1890, 1897, 1904.
Mars,   1877, 1884, 1891, 1898, 1905.
The Sun,   1878, 1885, 1892, 1899, 1906.
Venus,   1879, 1886, 1893, 1900, 1907.

CYCLE OF MARS (1909—1944)

Mars,   1909, 1916, 1923, 1930, 1937, 1944.
The Sun,   1910, 1917, 1924, 1931, 1938.
   etc.   etc.

In the cycles presented above, the planets
preside over the years set opposite their
names. The student can easily construct
the cycles preceding or following those
given.

CHAPTER X

YEARLY HOROSCOPES

As the Zodiac makes a complete revolution in 12 years, the sign under which a person was born, will be:

In House I. during the years 1, 13, 25, 37, 49, 61, 73, 85, 97, 109, etc., of the person's life.

In House XII. during the years 2, 14, 26, 38, 50, 62, 74, 86, 98.

In House XI. during the years 3, 15, 27, 39, 51, 63, 75, 86, 99.

In House X. during the years 4, 16, 28, 40, 52, 64, 76, 88, 100.

In House IX. during the years 5, 17, 29, 41, 53, 65, 77, 89.

In House VIII. during the years 6, 18, 30, 42, 54, 66, 78, 90.

In House VII. during the years 7, 19, 31, 43, 55, 67, 79, 91.

In House VI. during the years 8, 20, 32, 44, 56, 68, 80, 92.

In House V. during the years 9, 21, 33, 45, 57, 69, 81, 93.

In House IV. during the years 10, 22, 34, 46, 58, 70, 82, 94.

In House III. during the years 11, 23, 35, 47, 59, 71, 83, 95.

In House II. during the years 12, 24, 36, 48, 60, 72, 84, 96.

This change is due to the fact that the Zodiac moves around by 30°, one whole sign, every year. If Leo, for instance, was in House I. at the birth of a person, it will be there again in his 37th year. In his 45th year Aries will be in House I. This is figured as follows:

$$45 - 1 = 44. \quad 44 \div 12 = 3, \text{ remainder, 8.}$$
Add 5, the number of Leo. $8 + 5 = 13.$
$13 - 12 = 1$, the number of Aries.

When the Sign of Nativity returns to House I.—Here you simply interpret the sign according to its general meaning as given in chapters 3 and 4. In our next lesson we shall study the meanings of the other Signs of the Zodiac passing through House I.

When the Sign of Nativity passes through House XII.—Obstacles to all enterprises, animosities difficult to overcome, illnesses, bad year for traveling or for beginning business or starting a law suit. Betrayal by friends.

When the Sign of Nativity passes through

House XI.—Anxieties, threatened loss of reputation; the death of a friend or relative interferes with one's prospects, but powerful protections will save the day. Probabilities of travel.

When the Sign of Nativity passes through House X.—A favorable year for any business having money-making as its object. A good time to take a sea voyage or to attack and conquer one's enemies. Fame will come to the subject. Also a chance to marry well. These excellent omens will be darkened by a family mourning.

When the Sign of Nativity passes through House IX.—Another excellent year for all matters of affection and friendship. Also for the success of enterprises and the effective assistance of people in high position. Threatened loss of most of these good things through some scandalous revelation coming to ears it should not reach.

When the Sign of Nativity passes through House VIII.—Illnesses and even danger of death. Betrayal by friends and disastrous love affairs. Those you liked best will turn out to be your worst enemies; to a great extent it will be your own fault.

When the Sign of Nativity passes through House VII.—Danger of robbery and fire.

5

Favorable year for entering upon married life. Unpleasant relations with one's superiors or employers. Great changes in the subject's position.

When the Sign of Nativity passes through House VI. — Dangerous illness. Great struggles. Annoying and lasting enmities. More than modest financial circumstances. The subject ought to be on his guard against everybody and everything. Wounds of a serious character.

When the Sign of Nativity passes through House V.—Danger from perfidious enemies, but happy chances through the protection of people in high position. Probable marriage. Providential assistance in the nick of time. The occupation of the subject will be the cause of successful travels.

When the Sign of Nativity passes through House IV.—Inheritance, or large present made to the subject. Danger of a serious fall or of drowning while on a business trip. A lucky year for the enterprises the subject will undertake alone, but he must not count on any assistance or any useful influence exerted in his favor. Family journeys. Unfortunate complications in love affairs.

When the Sign of Nativity passes through

House III.—A year of traveling or at least of moving. Threatened secret enmities and slow diseases. Loss of confidence on the part of the subject's employers. Financial failure. Friends will forsake him. He will be the victim of constant persecutions on the part of envious people bent on ruining his career.

When the Sign of Nativity passes through House II.—A splendid year for the financial prospects of the subject, except that he will be particularly exposed to being robbed or swindled. Those he has a right to believe his best friends will turn out his enemies. Danger through four-footed animals. Position due to influential protectors. Chance offered the subject to undertake a long and profitable journey. Physical dangers threaten the subject and his or her spouse.

THE PLANETS AS SEEN THROUGH A TELESCOPE

CHAPTER XI

MEANINGS OF THE PLANETS IN THE SOLAR HOUSES

The student understands clearly that the position of the Houses never varies; House I. always occupying the space devoted to the Zodiacal Sign Aries in our *original* design of the Zodiacal Circle on page 16, while the Zodiacal Sign of Nativity must be placed in this House I. in each particular case. For a thorough understanding of this all-important principle I refer you once more to Chapter V. which clearly explains the various points at issue. Now I propose to go one step further in my brief course of practical tuition and give you a concise synopsis of the "Meanings of each Planet when found in each House."

1. SATURN

In House I.—Delicate constitution, poor health, slow intelligence, gloomy disposition, dislike for social intercourse. In House II.—Very commonplace life-work, up-hill efforts to doubtful success. In House III.—Quarrels with relatives on account of money matters especially about inheritances. In House IV.—Vicious tendencies, miserliness, meanness in all affairs of life. In House V.—Childlessness, or loss of children in babyhood. In House VI.— Chronic diseases and needy circumstances. In House VII.— Unfortunate for partnerships and marriage. In House VIII.—A low, dangerous nature; will end his or her life in prison or even on the gallows. In House IX.—The genius of the inventor, the discoverer, the explorer; a powerful mind but seldom for the good of others or his own. In House X.— High position or honors, obtained through unworthy, sometimes shameful, means. In House XI.— A tendency to practice usury and even worse traffics; a despicable character generally. In House XII. Hatred of one's fellow-beings which is returned in kind; a wretched ending to a contemptible life.

2. JUPITER

In House I.—Splendid health, sanguine nature, fine presence, power over others, success. In House II.—Taste for arts and sciences. Success in almost any career; the subject is often chosen for important public offices or to manage large enterprises, as he inspires confidence. In House III.—A leader in the family circle, generally succeeds in pushing his own people to excellent positions. In House IV.—Fortune made in mining or in large agricultural enterprises. Especially endowed as an engineer. In House V.—Happiness in love matters and marriage relations; perhaps too much fickleness in affections. Blessed in children. In House VI. — Very large wealth; superb estates, picture galleries, horses, yachts, etc. In House VII.—Rich marriage, but, whenever the aspects of the other planets are not favorable, unhappiness in a union contracted more through ambition than for love. In House VIII.—The fine omens of the planets will be darkened by law suits, calumnies, loss of protectors, etc. In House IX.—Fortune made by means of extended traveling at home and abroad. In House X.—High official positions. In House XI.—Many friends and many people under the subject's orders; success greatly due to influential relations. In House XII.—Most serious reverses from which the subject will emerge triumphant, ending his life prosperous and universally honored.

3. MARS

In House I. — Aggressive, quarrelsome disposition; all through life frequently the

victim of accident, wounds, falls, etc. In
House II.—The calling of the subject will
be of a dangerous nature; often he will be
in the army or navy. In House III.—Bitter
family quarrels. In House IV.—Severe
illnesses due to the subject's imprudence or
excesses. In House V.—Extreme sensuality,
resulting but too often in physical, financial
and social ruin. In House VI.—Heavy
losses of money caused by men or the elements, especially fire and water. In House
VII.—Unfortunate marriages, separations,
divorces, or, when the union is happy, early
bereavement. In House VIII.—Violent
accidents, serious wounds, even death. In
House IX.—Great taste for dangerous ex-
peditions, that may, and probably will, end
fatally. In House X.—The social position
of the subject will be ruined without warning. In House XI.—Frequent fights and
association with objectionable people. In
House XII.—Mars is here at its worst as it
may tempt the subject to commit murder,
or suicide.

4. THE SUN

In House I.—Noble instincts and healthy
ambition. Excellent constitution and long
life. In House II.—Honors and high situa-
tions coming to the subject on account of

his brain-work and his accomplishments. In House III.—An only son, or in every way superior to, and more successful than, his brothers. Prosperity and distinction in a foreign country. In House IV.—Conceit replaces pride; a love for show at any cost ruins the prospects of the subject. In House V.—Pure, noble and disinterested love; a scrupulously honest conscience; a progeny to be proud of. In House VI.—Large wealth, life spent in a sumptuous palace. In House VII.—A brilliant marriage will raise the position of the subject far above expectations. In House VIII.—High honors on the battlefield, or on account of deeds of heroism. If the other planets are unfavorable, death in a fire or by sunstroke. In House IX.—Brilliant intelligence, great social and financial success, wide fame. In House X.—Honors bestowed on the subject, governmental position, high promotion in the church. In House XI.—A leading position in society and great wealth coming. In House XII.—Ambitions far beyond possibilities of realization; reverses followed by recoveries, happy and comfortable old age.

5. VENUS

In House I.—Beauty, grace and the gift of pleasing, but no faculty to judge people right, and, on that account, frequent deceptions. In House II.—Riches coming through the other sex; talents for such trades as are devoted to the beautifying of the body or to the light recreation of the mind. In House III.—Promise of perfect harmony with one's family. In House IV.—The loving instinct of the subject will prove a cause of ruin on account of excesses or lack of constancy. In House V.—Tenderness, platonic love, disinterested devotion, beauty of body and soul, bliss in mutual love. In House VI.—Inheritance or large gift from a person of the other sex, close to you by the ties of love or blood. In House VII.—Most happy marriage. In House VIII.—Exasperated jealousy leading to crime, committed either by, or against, the subject. In House IX.—Ambition excited by love, the loved one met on a travel or belonging to another nationality. In House X.—Social prominence due to the efforts and influence of a loved one. In House XI.—Innumerable flirtations, but generally helpful in one's career. In House XII.—Contemptible

love affairs, position ruined through unworthy intrigues.

6. MERCURY

In House I.—Great versatility but very
superficial talents; ability in handling
people; the other planets will decide
whether this cleverness will prove a bless-
ing or a curse. In House II.—Versatility is
here still more marked and so are its draw-
backs. In House III.—The subject will be
in partnership with brother or sister. In
House IV.—Serious illnesses, low occupations, wretched understanding of life. In
House V.—A disposition to be unscrupulous
in all dealings. In House VI.—The subject
will be a broker of some kind, a speculator
with other people's money, generally lucky
but seldom honest. In House VII.—Two
successive marriages or sometimes two
simultaneous households. In House VIII.
—A quarrelsome disposition; going to law
on the slightest pretext and seldom faithful
to his word. In House IX.—Love for
traveling and the society of foreigners;
constant changes in plans. In House X.—
Great, but unwarranted, ambitions, rewarded
only by minor positions. In House XI.—
Many useful acquaintances but few real

friends. In House XII.—Many disasters due to the lack of wisdom and the intriguing ways of the subject. Threats of prison, exile and total ruin.

7. THE MOON

In House I.—Queer tastes, disposition to constant changes. In House II.—A number of successive occupations, lack of stability in pursuits. In House III.—Twin brothers or sisters, early death of mother, many travels in one's own country. In House IV.—Accidents on the water, danger of drowning, possible insanity, sudden changes of position. In House V.—Fickleness in love matters and lack of moral principles; often childishness. In House VI.— One lives under the persistent illusion of being rich, frequently in the train of some wealthy protector. In House VII.—Unlucky marriages. Very frequently separations or divorces. In House VIII.— Threatened fatal ending of life on the water or near the water on account of the hatred of persons of the opposite sex. In House IX.—Extended traveling in foreign countries, often exile and death away from home. In House X.—Upsetting of excellent prospects through the wayward or wicked conduct of the subject. The reputation will be tarnished and the life made wretched and restless. In House XI.—Undesirable associations and bad habits ruining the chances of the subject. In House XII.—The worst of all combinations. Applies to regular malefactors, wandering about looking for crimes to commit, or at least leading a life of dissipation amidst the lowest surroundings.

CHAPTER XII

CASTING A HOROSCOPE

The "Horoscope of Nativity" forecasts
the entire life of the subject, while the
"Horoscope of Revolution" gives information about a certain day, or month, or year.
The difference between the two is marked,
and we will state the points in which the
manner of casting a "Horoscope of Revolution" varies from the other, in a footnote,*
for future reference.

At present we will proceed, without delay,
to cast a Horoscope of Nativity.

In our system now presented for the

---

*HOROSCOPE OF REVOLUTION

For the *summit* of the genethliac scale add the Fatidic
number to the year in question.

In consulting the Zodiacal Calendar and the cyclic tables
look for the year in question.

Orient (locate) the Zodiac according to instructions on
pages 129 and 130.

For *locating the planets* consult the circle of the Rose-
Cross (page 184), disregarding the table of Arcanes, page
167.

Otherwise follow closely the method employed in this
chapter.

first time to the American public, one of the essential elements of every horoscope consists of the name of the person of whom the horoscope is cast. By name we mean "the given name and the family name." To this must be added the exact date of birth, including hour, date, month and year. Should the subject be born before mid-day then he is supposed, astrologically, to be born on the preceding day and his horoscope is based on that date and not on the date which he generally believes to be that of his birth.

Now, to make our instructions in the matter perfectly simple and clear, let us take an example, and choose the Horoscope of a very prominent man, so that the reader may judge for himself whether the results of this horoscope correspond with what we know of that man's life.

We will choose for the erection of what is called technically a GENETHLIAC FIGURE, Victor Hugo, the great French poet, born before mid-day on February 26, 1802.

The first operation consists in translating into numbers every letter found in the name and surname of the illustrious Frenchman. Here is the

TABLE OF NUMBERS REPRESENTED BY LETTERS

A	= 1.	N	= 5, or 50.
B	= 2.	O	= 7, or 70.
C	= 2, or 20.	P	= 8, or 80.
D	= 4.	Q	= 1, or 100.
E	= 5.	R	= 2, or 200.
F	= 8, or 80.	S	= 3, or 300.
G	= 3.	T	= 4, or 400.
H	= 8.	TS	= 9, or 90.
TH	= 9.	U	= 6.
I	= 1, or 10.	V	= 6.
J	= 1, or 10.	W	= 6.
K	= 2, or 20.	X	= 6, or 60.
L	= 3, or 30.	Y	= 1, or 10.
M	= 4, or 40.	Z	= 7.

This transformation of the letters of the alphabet into numbers is not arbitrary, but proceeds from the books of the Kabbala and the traditions of the Rosicrucians.* If I were to introduce here the Hebrew alphabet, I could make this interesting and important part much clearer to the student. But this would lead too far, and it is sufficient for him to know the value of each letter in figures.

Now that you know the numerical value of the letters you will arrange the letters forming the given name in one column;

*A supposed secret society "of the rose-cross," described in a book published in 1614.

then beginning at the bottom, you will place
1 opposite the lowest letter, 2 opposite the
letter above and so on until you reach the
top. You multiply this first figure, in each
case, with the number representing the letter and you add the products of all these
multiplications.

As an example, here is how the calculation will look when applied to the name of
"Victor":

$$V - 6 \times 6 = 36$$
$$I - 1 \times 5 = 5$$
$$C - 2 \times 4 = 8$$
$$T - 4 \times 3 = 12$$
$$O - 7 \times 2 = 14$$
$$R - 2 \times 1 = 2$$

Victor............77

Let us repeat the same operation for the
family name:

$$H - 8 \times 4 = 32$$
$$U - 6 \times 3 = 18$$
$$G - 3 \times 2 = 6$$
$$O - 7 \times 1 = 7$$

Hugo............63

No attention is to be paid to any name
but the *given name* by which the subject was
most generally known since infancy, and to
the *family name* that he or she inherited
from the parents. It is impossible to base
a horoscope on pet names or adopted sur-

nam€s.   They must be really the name **and**
surname given to the little one when it came
into this world.

Now we have to transform the date of
birth into the proper degree of the sign of
the Zodiac under which the subject was
born. The Zodiacal Calender, found on page
117, will tell us that the 26th of February
corresponds to the 7th degree of the Constellation of "Pisces," which is the 12th Sign
of the Zodiac.   Now, if the reader refers to
our chapter on Cycles he will find that the
year 1802 was ruled by the planet "Mercury." (See page 127.)

Now let us put all our information down
in a line.

77 — 63 — 12 — 7   Mercury.

Of course, the reader remembers that the
Zodiacal sign under which the subject was
born must always be placed in House I. of
the Horoscope and all the other signs inscribed in their regular rotation within each
of the Solar Houses.

We now come to the building up of the
Genethliac Scale, by writing first the Year of
Nativity, then the Number of the Sign, then
the Degree, then the Total given by the
Name, then the Total given by the Sur-
name, finally the Number called "the Sum-

mit of the Horoscope," which is obtained as follows: Add all the digits contained in the name, surname, degree and sign,

$$7+7+6+3+7+1+2 = 33$$

This number (33) is called the *fatidic number*. We add it to the birthyear to get the summit of the horoscope:

$$1802 + 33 = 1835$$

Now, $1+8+3+5 = 17$. The two numbers, 33 and 17, refer to Arcanes XXXIII and XVII.

This first calculation gives us:

Year of Nativity.......................1802
No. of the Zodiacal Sign............... 12
Degree................................   7
Name.................................. 77
Surname 63
Summit of the Horoscope.............1835

Let us now reverse the order of these figures, making it read as follows:

Genethliac Scale of Victor Hugo.

Summit ....1835 — X.
Name .... 63 — XI.
Surname .... 77 — XII.
Degree ....   7 — I.
Sign of the Zodiac.... 12 — II.
Year of Nativity......1802 — III.

The Roman figures at the right hand of the above figures indicate the "Houses," over which the planets and arcanes exert an influence, which we shall find by consulting the "Fatidic Circles." Thus the

four indications furnished us by the figure
1835 will influence House X.; the two indications furnished us by the number 63 will
influence House XI., and so on, down to
House III.

We see that they will influence these
Houses, either *directly* by being placed in the
space reserved for each House, on the circle
of the Horoscope, or *indirectly* by means of
a *Ray* from the House where they will be
placed to the House which they are to influence. (See cut, page 153.)

Now that the Genethliac Scale has been
constructed and the Fatidic Circle selected,
we proceed as follows:

A circle being a figure without beginning
or end there must be a rule to find out
where to start it. A special table called
"Table of Starting Points" (p. 168) tells us,
according to the decade of Nativity, where
we shall find the first indication to be in-
serted in connection with House X.

We will continue with the example which
we have been using. The 7th degree of any
sign of the Zodiac belongs to its first decade, the Table in question shows us opposite the first decade of "Pisces" the Roman
figure LXXVIII. This is our starting
point and if we look in the Fatidic Circle,

No. 5, (p. 179) under the influence of Mercury, we find written the following:

200—10. LXXVIII. Saturn.

Which means that Saturn has to be
placed in House X.

Now, the Fatidic Circles contain the following numbers:

1, 2, 3, 4, 5, 6, 7, 8, 9, 10, 20, 30, 40, 50, 60,
70, 80, 90, 100, 200, 300, 400.

Therefore, all other numbers have to be
decomposed in their simple elements, thus:

1,000, 2,000, etc., become respectively 10,
20, and so on.

In the hundreds, all numbers above 400
are changed to the corresponding numbers
below 10. Thus: 500, 600, etc., become, respectively, 5, 6, etc.

As a complete example, let us take the
Summit of the Genethliac Scale we have
just erected for the Victor Hugo horoscope.

This Summit is 1835; it is thus decomposed: 1,000 becomes 10. 800 becomes 8.
30 remains 30. 5 remains 5.

Continuing to analyze the numbers of our
Genethliac Scale: The Name—63, gives 60
and 3. The Surname—77, gives 70 and 7.
The Degree—7, remains 7. The Sign—12,
gives 10 and 2. The year of Nativity—
1802, gives us 10, 8 and 2.

We have now all the various elements needed for building the Figure of our Horoscope. We take a compass and trace "three concentric circles" about the size of our illustration. We orient it (fix its bearings) by placing outside of these circles—which have been previously divided into twelve equal parts—the Roman figure I to the East, i. e., where Aries was placed in our first illustration in the Chapter on the Signs of the Zodiac. We proceed to number all the divisions, as we explained it in the Chapter on the Solar Houses. For, as you must know by this time, *the positions of the Houses never change.*

Next, we inscribe the Signs of the Zodiac, in their regular order, beginning with "Pisces," which is the Sign of Nativity of the subject whose Horoscope we are now casting.

Now comes the task of placing the Planets and the Arcana where they belong. We do it as follows:

The first number in our Genethliac Scale refers, as always, to House X. and will read as follows:

1835—or 10, 8, 30, 5.

We know that our Cycle is that of Mercury and our starting point LXXVIII.

We find that this, LXXVIII., just corresponds to 10, (the first division of our number, 1835,) and that, opposite, is inscribed

Saturn." We therefore inscribe the symbol of Saturn (♄) in House X.

The next figure is 8; to find what it corresponds to, we go to the *Table of the twenty-two Major Arcanes* (which has

always to be consulted *before* beginning any
of the Fatidic Circles, 1 to 7, inclusive).
We find that 8 corresponds to Major
Arcane VIII. and it tells us to place the
Symbol of Venus in the Sign of Cancer.
To show, however, that the House X is the
one influenced, we direct a Ray from Cancer
to House X, being careful to mark the
starting point of the Ray with a small circle
to indicate where it comes from. We also
inscribe the Roman figure belonging to the
Arcane, and do so all along whenever we
meet with Major Arcanes, as these are of
such capital importance.

The next figure is 30, which, on the
Table of Major Arcanes, we find in connection with Arcane XII. and with the mention, "The Moon in Libra." We place the
symbol of the Moon in Libra with a Ray to
House X., and, also in Libra the figure XII.

The last figure of the first number is 5.
We follow the Table of Major Arcanes to
the end, and then start at the beginning of
Fatidic Circle No. 5, devoted to Mercury,
until we meet, for the first time, figure 5.
Opposite we read "Mercury in Aries," and,
therefore, we place the symbol of Mercury
in Aries with a Ray to House X. We will
present our results in a table, as follows:

Cycle : MERCURY.   Starting Point : LXXVIII.

1835 for HOUSE X. ♐	10—Saturn [♄] in Sagittarius. 8—Venus [♀] in Cancer, with Major Arcane VIII. and a Ray to Sagittarius. 30—The Moon [☽] in Libra, with Major Arcane XII. and a Ray to Sagittarius. 5—Mercury [☿] in Aries, and a Ray to Sagittarius.
63 for HOUSE XI. ♑	60—The Sun [☉] in Sagittarius, with a Ray to Capricorn. 3—Venus [♀] in Capricorn.
77 for HOUSE XII. ♒	70—Mercury [☿] in Capricorn, with a Ray to Aquarius. 7—Mercury [☿] in Aquarius.
7 for HOUSE I. ♓	7—The Sun [☉] in Gemini, with a Ray to Pisces, and with Major Arcane VII.
12 for HOUSE II. ♈	10—Mercury [☿] in Virgo, with Major Arcane X. and with a Ray to Aries. 2—The Moon [☽] in Aries.
1802 for HOUSE III. ♉	10—Jupiter [♃] in Virgo, with a Ray to Taurus. 8—Jupiter [♃] in Cancer, with a Ray to Taurus. 2—Mars [♂] in Libra, with a Ray to Taurus

CONDENSED INTERPRETATION

as revealed by the presence of the Zodiacal Signs and Planets in each of the Solar Houses (Chaps. III., IV., V., XI.), by the Aspects (Chap. VIII.) and by the Arcanes (end of this Chap.).

HOUSE I. Fame in literature through unremitting labors. Dreamy, poetical temperament; restless and changeable disposition; refined but pleasure-loving tastes. Wealth and honors. Ripe old age. (V. H., one of the greatest French poets and authors, died at the age of 84. See Houses II., X.)

HOUSE II. Marked versatility; lack of stability. High position; threatened loss of it. Property through marriage. (V. H. was created viscount and life member of French Senate, but was extremely changeable in his political views. See House VII.)

HOUSE III. Family troubles; long journeys in consequence; strife and contention between relatives. (V. H.'s father and mother separated, father taking children.)

HOUSE IV. Parents of excellent family. Father high rank in army. Subject con-

ceited: fond of show and applause. (V. H.'s
father was a general in French army. V. H.
was exceedingly vain and craved public
applause.)

HOUSE V. Honors and distinctions. Possible flirtations. Happy marriage. Children
affectionate—girl causes anxiety; disaster
threatened. (V. H. married for love; fairly
worshiped his wife. See House VIII.)

HOUSE VI. Loss of eldest child. Troubles
with dependents. (See House VIII.)

HOUSE VII. Fateful events; 'loss of position; changeable fortunes; ultimate triumph.
Rich marriage. (V. H. elected to Academy,
1841; in political exile from 1848 to 1870.
See House II.)

HOUSE VIII. Violent and probably *fatal
accident* on water; threatened ending of
child's life; warning of *insanity* and *close
connection* between it and *death*. (One of V.
H.'s daughters and her husband were
drowned in a boating accident and another
daughter became insane in consequence.)

HOUSE IX. At enmity with the church.
Lack of religious feeling. (Witness his
writings.)

HOUSE X. Happiness, save sorrows
through children. Mother's influence inimical. Many years *prisoner or exile*. Many

friends. *Highest governmental honors.* (At his funeral France conferred highest national honors on V. H. See Houses VII., VIII.)

HOUSE XI. Early vicissitudes; changeable friendships; risks from intrigue; brother or sister unfriendly. Final triumph. (V. H.'s youth was marked by frequent changes of environment. See Houses III., VII.)

HOUSE XII. Quarrels with friends. *Exile for political reasons.* Renown in liberal arts. (See Houses VII., I., II., X.)

(Note especially the several marked indications of *renown, exile,* early vicissitudes and death of child.)

———

For further practice we will give as another sample the actual horoscope of a personal friend. (For obvious reasons, the name is withheld.)

First name, 102; Family Name, 31; Birth, December 7, 1847, in the morning. Result:

$$102 - 31 - 15 - 9 \text{ Venus.}$$
$$1 + 0 + 2 + 3 + 1 + 1 + 5 + 9 = 22.$$
$$1847 + 22 = 1869.$$

———

☞ Remember that middle names are *disregarded* in the erection of a horoscope.

Information from the above: 1, the fatidic number 22 refers to Arcane XXII., forecasting great fatality. 2, The summit of the Horoscope means Arcane XXIV. (1 + 8 + 6 + 9 = 24), making the success of the subject dependent on a woman. 3, The second decan of Sagittarius (see Page 113) corroborates Arcane XXII. and makes the subject of angry, gloomy temper, scientifically inclined, frank and impressionable 4. The Moon reigning over the second decan of Sagittarius (see Page 115) indicates that the troubles and perils arise from marriage. 5, The 15th degree of Sagittarius announces timidity.

We continue the erection of the horoscope:

	Summit............................	1869 —	X
	Name	31 —	XI
Genethliac Scale	Surname.........................	102 —	XII
of N. N.	Degree	15 —	I
	Sign of the Zodiac	9 --	II
	Year of Nativity............	1847 —	III

Starting, in the Fatidic Circle of Venus (Page 182) from the second decan of Sagittarius, Arcane LXXVIII., we construct the figure shown in our cut. (The student should remember that, in counting, Arcane *I.* (not 22) follows upon Arcane 78.)

House X.—1869.

1000 = 10—Saturn—In Virgo.
800 = 8—Arcane VIII. and Venus in Cancer, and ray to X.

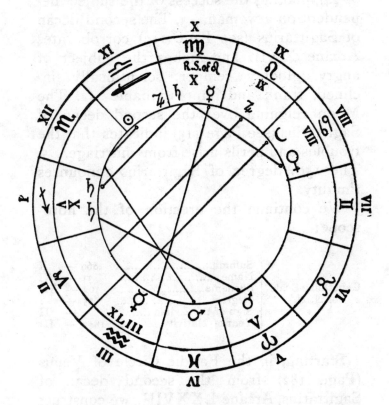

60—Arcane XV. and Saturn in Sagittarius, and ray to X
9—The Royal Star of Leo.

House XI.—31.

30—Jupiter in Libra.
1—Arcane LV. of the Rose-Cross:
The Sword.

House XII.—102

1 ᴏᴏ—Mars in Pisces, and ray to XII.
2—The Sun in Libra (with Jupiter),
and ray to XII.

House I.—15.

10—Saturn.
5—Arcane 5, with Mars in Aries
(ray to I.).

House II.—9.

9—Arcane IX. with Jupiter in Leo
(ray to II.)

House III.—1847.

1000 = 10—Arcane X. with Mercury in Virgo
(ray to III.).
800 = 8—The Moon in Cancer (ray to III.)
40—The minor Arcane XLIII.
7—Mercury, and ray from X. to III.

☞ If by accident any planet is not located, put it on its
diurnal or nocturnal throne (see page 79), according to the
time of birth.

The meaning of the Zodiacal Sign inscribed in each House is easily gathered from Chapter III. by consulting Chapter V.; but the student will welcome the detailed interpretation of the Planets (see Chap. XI.) and of their Aspects (see Chap. VIII.), which follows:

Saturn, twice in House I.—Poverty and hard work in youth; independent spirit, melancholy temperament.

Saturn in House X.—Nocturnal birth makes settled position difficult till thirtieth year. Endangers married happiness and children.

Saturn in Virgo.—Mysterious fatalities, which concern position because of Virgo being in House X. Loss of grown children. Taste for science and public life. Two marriages possible.

Saturn in Sagittarius.—Slow to learn. Mind hard to understand. Sorrows in wedlock. Good morals. High promotion late, if ever.

Saturn with Mercury in the same House (X.).—Concentration of character, deliberate, grave, discreet. Weakness in the tests of life. Serious study.

Saturn with the Royal Star of Leo (which is as powerful as the Sun).—Strong reasoning power, but slowness in learning. Danger of losing position.

Saturn in aspect of opposition with Mars.—Peaceful mind, poor fighter. Domestic enemies. Serious illness. Great disasters.

Jupiter in House XI.—Influential friends. Fortunate relations. Success in enterprises. Promotion. Early marriage and first child a boy.

Jupiter in Libra.—Justice, good conscience, good morals. Favor of the great. A happy second marriage.

Jupiter with Sun.—Rise above the station of parents. Honors, riches, fame.

Jupiter with Arcane of Sword.—The good things foretold will not be obtained except through hard fight.

Jupiter in trine aspect with Mercury. (Favorable; see Page 126).—Keen judgment. Talent for science and arts. Ingenuity. Wealth and honors.

Jupiter in square aspect with the Moon.—Instability of wealth and position. Friendship of the great. Protection from enemies.

Jupiter in opposition to Mars.—Friendship changing to enmity. Marital troubles. Separation from family or children.

Mars in House IV.—Misfortune caused by women. Danger of wounds by steel or fire. Falls from high places. Brain disease, headaches. Troubles with parents or parents-in-law.

Mars in House V.—Separation from children, harmful to them. Danger arising from occupation. Illegitimate children.

Mars in Aries.—Irritable temper. Wounds in head. Trouble with eyes and intestines.

Mars in Pisces.—Great struggles for a competency or a fortune. Persecution, slander. Sorrow in love affairs. Separation from children. Poverty of parents. Passionate temper.

Mars in trine aspect with Venus.—Constant activity with good results. Pride. Inconsistency.

Mars in trine aspect with the Moon.—Diseases, vicissitudes during a trip.

Mars in opposition with Mercury.—Bad connections. Danger of imprisonment.

The Sun in House XI.—High, useful protection. Taste for art. Good reputation. Old age happier than youth.

The Sun in Libra.—Great moral qualities. Reflective, observing mind. Talent for poetry and the arts.

The Sun together with the Sword.—Late honor, after hard fights.

The Sun in trine aspect with Mercury. —Fame as a scientist or inventor.

The Sun in square aspect with Venus.— Wealth and honors due to a woman. Many friends.

Venus in House VIII.—Childless marriage. Early end of married life.

Venus in Cancer.—Fickle in love. Widowhood or separation. Love affair on a journey.

Venus together with the Moon.—Unsettled marriage. Two love affairs at the same time.

Mercury in House III.—Inventive and observative mind. Wide information. Fame in science or literature.

Mercury in House X.—High connections. Independent spirit. Talent for art and mathematics.

Mercury in Virgo.—Talent for science. Eloquence. Philosophies. Some great adversities.

Mercury in Aquarius. — Serious, deep study in occult matters. Good observer and quick to learn. Road to a fortune through science or the arts.

Mercury in sextile aspect with the Moon. —Talent for the arts and for business.

The Moon in House VIII.—Journeys not

profitable. Dangerous to persons of the other sex. Wealth through public favor or from unexpected quarter.

The Moon in Cancer.—Good conscience. Sensitiveness. Superior nature. Frequent journeys. Honors acquired by work. Vivid imagination.

The general result to be gathered from the above mass of information would be as follows:

"The subject, child of poor parents, was not happy in his youth; his talents and his power of accommodating himself to circumstances served him to rise in spite of many serious obstacles and dangerous enemies; by the aid of powerful friends he may attain to fame in the arts or in science."

Practice in weighing the values of the various items of information will enable the student to arrive at more precise and detailed results.

TABLE OF THE TWENTY-TWO MAJOR ARCANES

NUM-BERS.	AR-CANES.	SIGNS.	PLANETS	INTERPRETATIONS.
1	I	—	Moon	Creative will. Mysterious happenings in process of formation.
2	II	—	Venus	Antagonism. Division. Struggles on account of women.
3	III	—	Jupiter	Perfect love. Harmony. Marriage. Large families. Activity.
4	IV	—	Mars	Realization. Accomplished, fixed, durable results. Protections.
5	V	Aries	Mars	Struggles. Sufferings. Fire. Bad inspirations. Anger.
6	VI	Taurus	Moon	Indecision about marriage. Danger of seduction or adultery.
7	VII	Gemini	Sun	Great triumph. Honors, fame, success of all kinds.
8	VIII	Cancer	Venus	Moral debts. Contestations. Ruptures. Separations. Law-suits.
9	IX	Leo	Jupiter	Merited honors. Hard-won experience.
10	X	Virgo	Mercury	Fateful events. The proud abased and the humble elevated.
20	XI	—	Mars	Success through some daring venture. Obstacles overcome.
30	XII	Libra	Moon	Position lost suddenly. Violent death.
40	XIII	—	—	Disappointment in one's ambitions. Arcane of the destroyer.
50	XIV	—	Sun	Great danger in store if one lacks decision in the right time.
60	XV	Scorpio	Saturn	Predestination, especially concerning marriage and children.
70	XVI	Sagittarius	Jupiter	Ruin of position. Loss of future. Catastrophe.
80	XVII	Capricorn	Mercury	Arcane of Hope; favorable or not, according to other indications.
90	XVIII	—	Venus	Love affairs much opposed. Hidden dangers. False security.
100	XIX	Aquarius	Venus	Great wealth; brilliant match; high honors; fame.
200	XX	Pisces	Jupiter	Fatal destiny. Delays and obstacles constantly recurring.
300	XXI	—	Saturn	High position in accordance with one's natural surroundings.
400	XXII	—	Sun	Foolish presumption. Success followed by failure. Ambush.

TABLE OF THE STARTING POINTS ON THE FATIDIC CIRCLES.

ARIES
- 1st Decan start from Arcane XXXVI.
- 2nd " " " " XXXVI.
- 3rd " " " " LXIV.

TAURUS
- 1st " " " " LXIV.
- 2nd " " " " XXXVI.
- 3rd " " " " XXXVI.

GEMINI
- 1st " " " " XXXVI.
- 2nd " " " " LXIV.
- 3rd " " " " XXXVI.

CANCER
- 1st " " " " XXXVI.
- 2nd " " " " XL.
- 3rd " " " " LXIV.

LEO
- 1st " " " " LXIV.
- 2nd " " " " XXXVI.
- 3rd " " " " XL.

VIRGO
- 1st " " " " XL.
- 2nd " " " " LXIV.
- 3rd " " " " XXXVI.

LIBRA . . . . . . {
1st Decan start from Arcane L.
2nd " " " " LXIV.
3rd " " " " LXXVIII.

SCORPIO . . . . {
1st " " " " LXXVIII.
2nd " " " " L.
3rd " " " " LXIV.

SAGITTARIUS . . {
1st " " " " LXIV.
2nd " " " " LXXVIII
3rd " " " " L.

CAPRICORN . . . {
1st " " " " L.
2nd " " " " LXXVIII.
3rd " " " " LXXVIII.

AQUARIUS . . . {
1st " " " " LXXVIII.
2nd " " " " L.
3rd " " " " LXXVIII.

PISCES . . . . . {
1st " " " " LXXVIII.
2nd " " " " LXXVIII.
3rd " " " " L.

I. THE FATIDIC CIRCLE OF SATURN

(Always begin with the 22 Major Arcanes.)

9	XXIII.	The Royal Star of Leo. (High protection. Celebrity.)
5	XXIV.	Saturn in Aries.
6	XXV.	Venus in Taurus.
7	XXVI.	Jupiter in Gemini.
1	XXVII.	The Arcane of the Scepter. (Successful enterprises. Authority given to the subject.)
2	XXVIII.	The Moon.
3	XXIX.	Venus.
4	XXX.	Jupiter.
5	XXXI.	Jupiter in Aries.
6	XXXII.	Mercury in Taurus.
7	XXXIII.	The Moon in Gemini.
8	XXXIV.	Mars in Cancer.
9	XXXV.	The Moon in Leo.
10	XXXVI.	The Sun in Virgo.
6	XXXVII.	The Royal Star of Taurus. (Union. Marriage. Protection of women.)
8	XXXVIII.	The Sun in Cancer.
9	XXXIX.	Saturn in Leo.
10	XL.	Jupiter in Lirgo.
20— 1	XLI.	Mars.
30— 2	XLII.	Venus in Libra.
40— 3	XLIII.	The Arcane of the Reaper. (The Emblem of failure and of things that never come to any satisfactory conclusion.)
50— 4	XLIV.	Jupiter in Scorpio.
60— 5	XLV.	Mercury in Sagittarius.

70— 6	XLVI.	The Moon in Capricorn.	
80— 7	XLVII.	Mercury.	
90— 8	XLVIII.	The Sun in Aquarius.	
100— 9	XLIX.	Saturn in Pisces.	
200—10	L.	Saturn.	
90	LI.	The Royal Star of Aquarius. (High situation due sometimes to a mere accident.)	
30	LII.	Mercury in Libra.	
50	LIII.	Mars in Scorpio.	
60	LIV.	The Sun in Sagittarius.	
1	LV.	The Arcane of the Sword. (Success in spite of all obstacles.)	
2	LVI.	The Moon.	
3	LVII.	Venus.	
4	LVIII.	Jupiter.	
5	LIX.	Mars in Aries.	
6	LX.	The Sun in Taurus.	
7	LXI.	Saturn in Gemini.	
8	LXII.	Venus in Cancer.	
9	LXIII.	Mercury in Leo.	
10	LXIV.	Mars in Virgo.	
50	LXV.	The Royal Star of Scorpio. (Dangers. Powerful enemies. Wounds.)	
70	LXVI.	Saturn in Capricorn.	
90	LXVII.	Venus in Aquarius.	
100	LXVIII.	Mercury in Pisces.	
20— 1	LXIX.	Crowned Mars. (A symbol of fortune.)	
30— 2	LXX.	The Moon in Libra.	
40— 3	LXXI.	The Symbol of the Reaper. (Danger for one's person and fortune.)	
50— 4	LXXII.	Saturn in Scorpio.	
60— 5	LXXIII.	Venus in Sagittarius.	
70— 6	LXXIV.	Jupiter in Capricorn.	
80— 7	LXXV.	Mercury.	
90— 8	LXXVI.	Mars in Aquarius.	
100— 9	LXXVII.	The Moon in Pisces.	
20—10	LXXVIII.	Saturn.	

II. THE FATIDIC CIRCLE OF JUPITER

(Always begin with the 22 Major Arcanes.)

9	XXIII.	The Royal Star of Leo. (High protection. Celebrity.)
5	XXIV.	Jupiter in Aries.
6	XXV.	Mercury in Taurus.
7	XXVI.	Mars in Gemini.
1	XXVII.	The Arcane of the Scepter. (Successful enterprises. Authority given to the subject.)
2	XXVIII.	The Moon.
3	XXIX.	Venus.
4	XXX.	Jupiter.
5	XXXI.	Mars in Aries.
6	XXXII.	The Moon in Taurus.
7	XXXIII.	Saturn in Gemini.
8	XXXIV.	The Sun in Cancer.
9	XXXV.	Saturn in Leo.
10	XXXVI.	Venus in Virgo.
6	XXXVII.	The Royal Star of Taurus. (Union. Marriage. Protection of women.)
8	XXXVIII.	Venus in Cancer.
9	XXXIX.	Jupiter in Leo.
10	XL.	Mars in Virgo.
20— 1	XLI.	Mars.
30— 2	XLII.	Mercury in Libra.
40— 3	XLIII.	The Arcane of the Reaper. (The Emblem of failure and of things that never come to any satisfactory conclusion.)
50— 4	XLIV.	Mars in Scorpio.
60— 5	XLV.	The Moon in Sagittarius.
70— 6	XLVI.	Saturn in Capricorn.

80— 7	XLVII.	Mercury.	
90— 8	XLVIII.	Venus in Aquarius.	
100— 9	XLIX.	Jupiter in Pisces.	
200—10	L.	Saturn.	
90	LI.	The Royal Star of Aquarius. (High situation due sometimes to mere accident.)	
30	LII.	The Moon in Libra.	
50	LIII.	The Sun in Scorpio.	
60	LIV.	Mercury in Sagittarius.	
1	LV.	The Arcane of the Sword. (Triumphant success in spite of all obstacles.)	
2	LVI.	The Moon.	
3	LVII.	Venus.	
4	LVIII.	Jupiter.	
5	LIX.	The Sun in Aries.	
6	LX.	Venus in Taurus.	
7	LXI.	Jupiter in Gemini.	
8	LXII.	Mercury in Cancer.	
9	LXIII.	The Moon in Leo.	
10	LXIV.	The Sun in Virgo.	
50	LXV.	The Royal Star of Scorpio. (Dangers. Powerful enemies. Wounds.)	
70	LXVI.	Jupiter in Capricorn.	
90	LXVII.	Mercury in Aquarius.	
'00	LXVIII.	The Moon in Pisces.	
20— 1	LXIX.	Crowned Mars. (A symbol of fortune.)	
30— 2	LXX.	Saturn in Libra.	
40— 3	LXXI.	The Symbol of the Reaper. (Danger for one's person and fortune.)	
50— 4	LXXII.	Jupiter in Scorpio.	
60— 5	LXXIII.	Mercury in Sagittarius.	
70— 6	LXXIV.	Mars in Capricorn.	
80— 7	LXXV.	Mercury.	
90— 8	LXXVI.	The Sun in Aquarius.	
100— 9	LXXVII.	Saturn in Pisces.	
20—10	LXXVIII	Saturn.	

III. THE FATIDIC CIRCLE OF MARS

(Always begin with the 22 Major Arcanes.)

9	XXIII.	The Royal Star of Leo. (High protection. Celebrity.)
5	XXIV.	Mars in Aries.
6	XXV.	The Moon in Taurus.
7	XXVI.	The Sun in Gemini.
1	XXVII.	The Arcane of the Scepter. (Successful enterprises. Authority given to the subject.)
2	XXVIII.	The Moon.
3	XXIX.	Venus.
4	XXX.	Jupiter.
5	XXXI.	The Sun in Aries.
6	XXXII.	Saturn in Taurus.
7	XXXIII.	Jupiter in Gemini.
8	XXXIV.	Venus in Cancer.
9	XXXV.	Jupiter in Leo.
10	XXXVI.	Mercury in Virgo.
6	XXXVII.	The Royal Star of Taurus. (Union. Marriage. Protection of women.)
8	XXXVIII.	Mercury in Cancer.
9	XXXIX.	Mars in Leo.
10	XL.	The Sun in Virgo.
20— 1	XLI.	Mars.
30— 2	XLII.	The Moon in Libra.
40— 3	XLIII.	The Arcane of the Reaper. (The Emblem of failure and of things that never come to any satisfactory conclusion.)
50— 4	XLIV.	The Sun in Scorpio.
60— 5	XLV.	Saturn in Sagittarius.
70— 6	XLVI.	Jupiter in Capricorn.

80— 7	XLVII.	Mercury.	
90— 8	XLVIII.	Mercury in Aquarius.	
100— 9	XLIX.	Mars in Pisces.	
200—10	L.	Saturn.	
90	LI.	The Royal Star of Aquarius. (High situation due sometimes to mere accident.)	
30	LII.	Saturn in Libra.	
50	LIII.	Venus in Scorpio.	
60	LIV.	Mercury in Sagittarius.	
1	LV.	The Arcane of the Sword. (Triumphant success in spite of all obstacles.)	
2	LVI.	The Moon.	
3	LVII.	Venus.	
4	LVIII.	Jupiter.	
5	LIX.	Venus in Aries.	
6	LX.	Mercury in Taurus.	
7	LXI.	Mars in Gemini.	
8	LXII.	The Moon in Cancer.	
9	LXIII.	Saturn in Leo.	
10	LXIV.	Venus in Virgo.	
50	LXV.	The Royal Star of Scorpio. (Dangers. Powerful enemies. Wounds.)	
70	LXVI.	Mars in Capricorn.	
90	LXVII.	The Moon in Aquarius.	
100	LXVIII.	Saturn in Pisces.	
20— 1	LXIX.	Mars. (A symbol of fortune.)	
30— 2	LXX.	Jupiter in Libra.	
40— 3	LXXI.	The Symbol of the Reaper. (Danger for one's person and fortune.)	
50— 4	LXXII.	Mars in Scorpio.	
60— 5	LXXIII.	The Moon in Sagittarius.	
70— 6	LXXIV.	The Sun in Capricorn.	
80— 7	LXXV.	Mercury.	
90— 8	LXXVI.	Venus in Aquarius.	
100— 9	LXXVII.	Jupiter in Pisces	
20—10	LXXVIII.	Satu...	

IV. THE FATIDIC CIRCLE OF THE SUN

(Always begin with the 22 Major Arcanes.)

9	XXIII.	The Royal Star of Leo. (High protection. Celebrity.)
5	XXIV.	The Sun in Aries.
6	XXV.	Saturn in Taurus.
7	XXVI.	Venus in Gemini.
1	XXVII.	The Arcane of the Scepter. (Successful enterprises. Authority given to the subject.)
2	XXVIII.	The Moon.
3	XXIX.	Venus.
4	XXX.	Jupiter.
5	XXXI.	Venus in Aries.
6	XXXII.	Jupiter in Taurus.
7	XXXIII.	Mars in Gemini.
8	XXXIV.	Mercury in Cancer.
9	XXXV.	Mars in Leo.
10	XXXVI.	The Sun in Virgo.
6	XXXVII.	The Royal Star of Taurus. (Union. Marriage. Protection of women.)
8	XXXVIII.	The Moon in Cancer.
9	XXXIX.	The Sun in Leo.
10	XL.	Venus in Virgo.
20— 1	XLI.	Mars.
30— 2	XLII.	Saturn in Libra.
40— 3	XLIII.	The Arcane of the Reaper. (The Emblem of failure and of things that never come to any satisfactory conclusion.)
50— 4	XLIV.	Venus in Scorpio.
60— 5	XLV.	Jupiter in Sagittarius.
70— 6	XLVI.	Mars in Capricorn.

FATIDIC CIRCLES

80— 7	XLVII.	Mercury	
90— 8	XLVIII.	The Moon in Aquarius.	
100— 9	XLIX.	The Sun in Pisces.	
200—10	L.	Saturn.	
90	LI.	The Royal Star of Aquarius. (High situation due sometimes to mere accident.)	
30	LII.	Jupiter in Libra.	
50	LIII.	Mercury in Scorpio.	
60	LIV.	The Moon in Sagittarius.	
1	LV.	The Arcane of the Sword. (Triumphant success in spite of all obstacles.)	
2	LVI.	The Moon.	
3	LVII.	Venus.	
4	LVIII.	Jupiter.	
5	LIX.	Mercury in Aries.	
6	LX.	The Moon in Taurus.	
7	LXI.	The Sun in Gemini.	
8	LXII.	Saturn in Cancer.	
9	LXIII.	Jupiter in Leo.	
10	LXIV.	Mercury in Virgo.	
50	LXV.	The Royal Star of Scorpio. (Dangers. Powerful enemies. Wounds.)	
70	LXVI.	The Sun in Capricorn.	
90	LXVII.	Saturn in Aquarius.	
100	LXVIII.	Jupiter in Pisces.	
20— 1	LXIX.	Crowned Mars. (A symbol of fortune.)	
30— 2	LXX.	Mars in Libra.	
40— 3	LXXI.	The Symbol of the Reaper. (Danger for one's person and fortune.)	
50— 4	LXXII.	The Sun in Scorpio.	
60— 5	LXXIII.	Saturn in Sagittarius.	
70— 6	LXXIV.	Venus in Capricorn.	
80— 7	LXXV.	Mercury.	
90— 8	LXXVI.	Mercury in Aquarius.	
100— 9	LXXVII.	Mars in Pisces.	
20—10	LXXVIII.	Saturn.	

V. THE FATIDIC CIRCLE OF MERCURY

(Always begin with the 22 Major Arcanes.)

9	XXIII.	The Royal Star of Leo. (High protection. Celebrity.)
5	XXIV.	Mercury in Aries.
6	XXV.	Mars in Taurus.
7	XXVI.	The Moon in Gemini.
1	XXVII.	The Arcane of the Scepter. (Successful enterprises. Authority given to the subject.)
2	XXVIII.	The Moon.
3	XXIX.	Venus.
4	XXX.	Jupiter.
5	XXXI.	The Moon in Aries.
6	XXXII.	The Sun in Taurus.
7	XXXIII.	Venus in Gemini.
8	XXXIV.	Saturn in Cancer.
9	XXXV.	Venus in Leo.
10	XXXVI.	Jupiter in Virgo.
6	XXXVII.	The Royal Star of Taurus. (Union. Marriage. Protection of women.)
8	XXXVIII.	Jupiter in Cancer.
9	XXXIX.	Mercury in Leo.
10	XL.	The Moon in Virgo.
20— 1	XLI.	Mars.
30— 2	XLII.	Mars in Libra.
40— 3	XLIII.	The Arcane of the Reaper. (The Emblem of failure and of things that never come to any satisfactory conclusion.)
50— 4	XLIV.	The Moon in Scorpio.
60— 5	XLV.	The Sun in Sagittarius.
70— 6	XLVI.	Venus in Capricorn.

80— 7	XLVII.	Mercury.	
90— 8	XLVIII.	Jupiter in Aquarius.	
100— 9	XLIX.	Mercury in Pisces.	
200—10	L.	Saturn.	
90	LI.	The Royal Star of Aquarius. (High situation due sometimes to mere accident.)	
30	LII.	The Sun in Libra.	
50	LIII.	Saturn in Scorpio.	
60	LIV.	Jupiter in Sagittarius.	
1	LV.	The Arcane of the Sword. (Triumphant success in spite of all obstacles.)	
2	LVI.	The Moon.	
3	LVII.	Venus.	
4	LVIII.	Jupiter.	
5	LIX.	Saturn in Aries.	
6	I.X.	Jupiter in Taurus.	
7	LXI.	Mercury in Gemini.	
8	LXII.	Mars in Cancer.	
9	LXIII.	The Sun in Leo.	
10	LXIV.	Saturn in Virgo.	
50	LXV.	The Royal Star of Scorpio. (Dangers. Powerful enemies. Wounds.)	
70	LXVI.	Mercury in Capricorn.	
90	LXVII.	Mars in Aquarius.	
100	LXVIII.	The Sun in Pisces.	
20— 1	LXIX.	Crowned Mars. (A symbol of fortune.)	
30— 2	LXX.	Venus in Libra.	
40— 3	LXXI.	The Symbol of the Reaper. (Danger for one's person and fortune.)	
50— 4	LXXII.	Mercury in Scorpio.	
60— 5	LXXIII.	Mars in Sagittarius.	
70— 6	LXXIV.	The Moon in Capricorn.	
80— 7	LXXV.	Mercury.	
90— 8	LXXVI.	Saturn in Aquarius.	
100— 9	LXXVII.	Venus in Pisces.	
20—10	LXXVIII.	Saturn.	

VI. THE FATIDIC CIRCLE OF THE MOON

(Always begin with the 22 Major Arcanes.)

9	XXIII.	The Royal Star of Leo. (High protection. Celebrity.)
5	XXIV.	The Moon in Aries.
6	XXV.	The Sun in Taurus.
7	XXVI.	Saturn in Gemini.
1	XXVII.	The Arcane of the Scepter. (Successful enterprises. Authority given to the subject.)
2	XXVIII.	The Moon.
3	XXIX.	Venus.
4	XXX.	Jupiter.
5	XXXI.	Saturn in Aries.
6	XXXII.	Venus in Taurus.
7	XXXIII.	Mercury in Gemini.
8	XXXIV.	Jupiter in Cancer.
9	XXXV.	Mercury in Leo.
10	XXXVI.	Mars in Virgo.
6	XXXVII.	The Royal Star of Taurus. (Union. Marriage. Protection of women.)
8	XXXVIII.	Mars in Cancer.
9	XXXIX.	The Moon in Leo.
10	XL.	Saturn in Virgo.
20— 1	XLI.	Mars.
30— 2	XLII.	The Sun in Libra.
40— 3	XLIII.	The Arcane of the Reaper. (The Emblem of failure and of things that never come to any satisfactory conclusion.)
50— 4	XLIV.	Saturn in Scorpio.
60— 5	XLV.	Venus in Sagittarius.
70— 6	XLVI.	Mercury in Capricorn.

80— 7	XLVII.	Mercury.
90— 8	XLVIII.	Mars in Aquarius.
100— 9	XLIX.	The Moon in Pisces.
200—10	L.	Saturn.
90	LI.	The Royal Star of Aquarius. (High situation due sometimes to mere accident.)
30	LII.	Venus in Libra.
50	LIII.	Jupiter in Scorpio.
60	LIV.	Mars in Sagittarius.
1	LV.	The Arcane of the Sword. (Triumphant success in spite of all obstacles.)
2	LVI.	The Moon.
3	LVII.	Venus.
4	LVIII.	Jupiter.
5	LIX.	Jupiter in Aries.
6	LX.	Mars in Taurus.
7	LXI.	The Moon in Gemini.
8	LXII.	The Sun in Cancer.
9	LXIII.	Venus in Leo.
10	LXIV.	Jupiter in Virgo.
50	LXV.	The Royal Star of Scorpio. (Dangers. Powerful enemies. Wounds.)
70	LXVI.	The Moon in Capricorn.
90	LXVII.	The Sun in Aquarius.
100	LXVIII.	Venus in Pisces.
20— 1	LXIX.	Crowned Mars. (A symbol of fortune.)
30— 2	LXX.	Mercury in Libra.
40— 3	LXXI.	The Symbol of the Reaper. (Danger for one's person and fortune.)
50— 4	LXXII.	The Moon in Scorpio.
60— 5	LXXIII.	The Sun in Sagittarius.
70— 6	LXXIV.	Saturn in Capricorn.
80— 7	LXXV.	Mercury.
90— 8	LXXVI.	Jupiter in Aquarius.
100— 9	LXXVII.	Mercury in Pisces.
20—10	LXXVIII.	Saturn.

VII. THE FATIDIC CIRCLE OF VENUS

(Always begin with the 22 Major Arcanes.)

9	XXIII.	The Royal Star of Leo. (High protection. Celebrity.)
5	XXIV.	Venus in Aries.
6	XXV.	Jupiter in Taurus.
7	XXVI.	Mercury in Gemini.
1	XXVII.	The Arcane of the Scepter. (Successful enterprises. Authority given to the subject.)
2	XXVIII.	The Moon.
3	XXIX.	Venus.
4	XXX.	Jupiter.
5	XXXI.	Mercury in Aries.
6	XXXII.	Mars in Taurus.
7	XXXIII.	The Sun in Gemini.
8	XXXIV.	The Moon in Cancer.
9	XXXV.	The Sun in Leo.
10	XXXVI.	Saturn in Virgo.
6	XXXVII.	The Royal Star of Taurus. (Union. Marriage. Protection of women.)
8	XXXVIII.	Saturn in Cancer.
9	XXXIX.	Venus in Leo.
10	XL.	Mercury in Virgo.
20— 1	XLI.	Mars.
30— 2	XLII.	Jupiter in Libra.
40— 3	XLIII.	The Arcane of the Reaper. (The Emblem of failure and of things that never come to any satisfactory conclusion.)
50— 4	XLIV.	Mercury in Scorpio.
60— 5	XLV.	Mars in Sagittarius.
⌐— 6	XLVI.	The Sun in Capricorn.

80— 7	XLVII.	Mercury.
90— 8	XLVIII.	Saturn in Aquarius.
100— 9	XLIX.	Venus in Pisces.
200—10	L.	Saturn.
90	LI.	The Royal Star of Aquarius. (High situation due sometimes to mere accident.)
30	LII.	Mars in Libra.
50	LIII.	The Moon in Scorpio.
60	LIV.	Saturn in Sagittarius.
1	LV.	The Arcane of the Sword. (Triumphant success in spite of all obstacles.)
2	LVI.	The Moon.
3	LVII.	Venus.
4	LVIII.	Jupiter.
5	LIX.	The Moon in Aries.
6	LX.	Saturn in Taurus.
7	LXI.	Venus in Gemini.
8	LXII.	Jupiter in Cancer.
9	LXIII.	Mars in Leo.
10	LXIV.	The Moon in Virgo.
50	LXV.	The Royal Star of Scorpio. (Dangers. Powerful enemies. Wounds.)
70	LXVI.	Venus in Capricorn.
90	LXVII.	Jupiter in Aquarius.
100	LXVIII.	Mars in Pisces.
20— 1	LXIX.	Crowned Mars. (A symbol of fortune.)
30— 2	LXX.	The Sun in Libra.
40— 3	LXXI.	The Symbol of the Reaper. (Danger for one's person and fortune.)
50— 4	LXXII.	Venus in Scorpio.
60— 5	LXXIII.	Jupiter in Sagittarius.
70— 6	LXXIV.	Mercury in Capricorn.
80— 7	LXXV.	Mercury.
90— 8	LXXVI.	The Moon in Aquarius.
100— 9	LXXVII.	The Sun in Pisces.
20—10	LXXVIII.	Saturn.

THE FATIDIC CIRCLE OF THE ROSE-CROSS

(The Major Arcanes are included in this Circle.)

1	I.	The Magus.
2	II.	Gate of Sanctuary. The Moon.
3	III.	Iris—Urania. Venus.
4	IV.	The Cubic Stone. Jupiter.
5	V.	Master of Arcanes. Mars in Aries.
6	VI.	The Two Ways. The Moon in Taurus.
7	VII.	Chariot of Osiris. Sun in Gemini.
8	VIII.	Balance and Sword. Venus in Cancer.
9	IX.	The Veiled Lamp. Jupiter in Leo.
10	X.	The Sphinx. Mercury in Virgo.
20	XI.	The Tamed Lion. Mars.
30	XII.	The Sacrifice. The Moon in Libra.
40	XIII.	The Reaping Skeleton.
50	XIV.	The Two Urns. The Sun in Scorpio.
60	XV.	Typhon. Saturn in Sagittarius.
70	XVI.	The Thunder Struck Tower. Jupiter in Capricorn.
80	XVII.	The Star of the Magi. Mercury.
90	XVIII.	The Twilight. Venus in Aquarius.
100	XIX.	The Dazzling Light. Jupiter in Pisces.
200	XX.	The Rising of the Dead. Saturn.
300	XXI.	The Crown of the Magi. The Sun.
400	XXII.	The Crocodile.
9	XXIII.	Master of Scepter. Royal Star of Leo.
5	XXIV.	Mistress of the Scepter. Mars in Aries.
6	XXV.	The Warrior of the Scepter. Mercury in Taurus.
7	XXVI.	Slave of Scepter. Jupiter in Gemini.
1	XXVII.	The Scepter.
2	XXVIII.	The Two Scepters. The Moon.
3	XXIX.	The Three Scepters. Venus.
4	XXX.	The Four Scepters. Jupiter.
5	XXXI.	The Five Scepters. The Sun in Aries.
6	XXXII.	The Six Scepters. Moon in Taurus.
7	XXXIII.	The Seven Scepters. Mars in Gemini.
8	XXXIV.	The Eight Scepters. Venus in Cancer.
9	XXXV.	The Nine Scepters. Saturn in Leo.
10	XXXVI.	The Ten Scepters. The Sun in Virgo.
6	XXXVII.	The Master of the Cups. The Royal Star of Taurus
8	XXXVIII.	The Mistress of the Cups. Mercury in Cancer.
9	XXXIX.	Warrior of the Cups. Jupiter in Leo.
10	XL.	Slave of the Cup. Venus in Virgo.

20— 1	XLI.	The Cup.
30— 2	XLII.	The Two Cups. The Moon in Libra.
40— 3	XLIII.	The Three Cups.
50— 4	XLIV.	The Four Cups. Mars in Scorpio.
60— 5	XLV.	Five Cups. Mercury in Sagittarius.
70— 6	XLVI.	The Six Cups. Jupiter in Capricorn.
80— 7	XLVII.	The Seven Cups. Mercury.
90— 8	XLVIII.	The Eight Cups. Venus in Aquarius.
100— 9	XLIX.	The Nine Cups. Saturn in Pisces.
200—10	L.	The Ten Cups. Saturn.
90	LI.	The Master of the Sword. The Royal Star of Aquarius.
30	LII.	Mistress of the Sword. Saturn in Libra.
50	LIII.	The Warrior of the Sword. The Sun in Scorpio.
60	LIV.	The Slave of the Sword. The Moon in Sagittarius.
1	LV.	The Sword.
2	LVI.	The Two Swords. The Moon.
3	LVII.	The Three Swords. Venus.
4	LVIII.	The Four Swords. Jupiter.
5	LIX.	The Five Swords. Venus in Aries.
6	LX.	The Six Swords. Saturn in Taurus.
7	LXI.	The Seven Swords. The Sun in Gemini.
8	LXII.	The Eight Swords. Moon in Cancer.
9	LXIII.	The Nine Swords. Mars in Leo.
10	LXIV.	The Ten Swords. Mercury in Virgo.
50	LXV.	The Master of the Pentacle. The Royal Star of Scorpio.
70	LXVI.	The Mistress of the Pentacle. Mars in Capricorn.
90	LXVII.	The Warrior of the Pentacle. Mercury in Aquarius.
100	LXVIII.	The Slave of the Pentacle. Jupiter in Pisces.
20— 1	LXIX.	The Crowned Pentacle. Mars.
30— 2	LXX.	The Two Pentacles. Jupiter in Libra.
40— 3	LXXI.	The Three Pentacles.
50— 4	LXXII.	The Four Pentacles. Venus in Scorpio.
60— 5	LXXIII.	The Five Pentacles. Saturn in Sagittarius.
70— 6	LXXIV.	The Six Pentacles. Sun in Capricorn.
80— 7	LXXV.	The Seven Pentacles. Mercury.
90— 8	LXXVI.	The Eight P't'cl's. Moon in Aquarius.
100— 9	LXXVII.	The Nine Pentacles. Mars in Pisces.
200—10	LXXVIII.	The Ten Pentacles. Saturn.

THE 22 MAJOR ARCANES

ARCANE I. (A = 1.) THE MAGUS

The Magus (magician) is standing in the attitude of the will-power about to act; he is dressed in white, the emblem of purity, with a circle of gold around his brow, emblem of eternal light; he holds in the right hand a scepter tipped with a circle, the emblem of creative intelligence. He raises this scepter toward Heaven to indicate his aspirations to wisdom, science and moral force. His left hand points towards the earth to show that he is ready to dominate over matter. In front of him, upon a cube —the image of absolute solidity—are found a cup full of human passions, a sword, the weapon of the braves who fight error, finally a golden pentacle (piece of money), the emblem of the reward granted to voluntary labor. His belt is a snake biting its tail, the symbol of eternity. The Ibis upon the cube typifies vigilance.

This Arcane, I., means: A firm will and confidence in yourself guided by reason and the love of justice shall lead you to the object of your ambition and save you from the dangers on the way.

ARCANE II. (B = 2.) THE GATE OF THE SANCTUARY

Here we have Occult Science represented by a stately woman seated between two columns of a temple, these columns representing Good and Evil; the figure is crowned with a crescent and her face is veiled, as a sign that Truth is not visible to the profane; she has upon her breast the Solar Cross, emblematic of universal generation, and, in her lap, a papyrus half covered by her cloak, indicating that the mysteries of the sacred science are unveiled only to the Initiated. The tiara upon her head is the emblem of the power of intelligence lighted up by wisdom represented by the crescent; the figure is seated, because science united to wisdom and will-power is immovable.

This Arcane, II., tells us that if man possesses a strong will he cannot fail to see the true light and to obey it properly. It is essential, however, that he should keep silent as to his opinions and projects, as it has been said that "the world belongs to the silent ones."

ARCANE III. (G = 3.) IRIS-URANIA

This is the ancient idea of Nature. It is represented by a woman seated upon a cube covered with eyes, the emblem of the visions of the famous seer, Hermes. Her feet rest upon a crescent of the moon, the emblem of matter subjected to mind. She is crowned with twelve stars representing the twelve months and the Sun serves her as a Nimbus, thus symbolizing the creative power of intelligence. In one hand she holds a scepter tipped with a globe, the emblem of her despotic action over the world; on her other hand is posed an eagle, its head turned towards her; this signifies the flight of the human soul returning to its initial principle: God.

This Arcane, III., means: That to wish for things possible is equivalent to creating them. To wish for things impossible is to prepare one's own ruin.

ARCANE IV. (D = 4.) THE CUBIC STONE

Here is a man bearing on his head a crowned helmet, the emblem of conquest, as the cube upon which he is sitting is the symbol of labor that has reached its completion. He holds the scepter of the Magi as a sign of the moral power acquired through sacred studies. His left hand, pointing downward, indicates the mastery over matter, while the dove on his breast symbolizes innocence, and his crossed legs signify the expansion of the power of human mind within the three dimensions of the Infinite: Height, Width, Depth. The cat upon the cube symbolizes the thought of the Magi who is able to see through the night of the ancient times.

This Arcane, IV., means that nothing resists a firm will-power which has for its lever the Knowledge of Truth and Justice. To fight for both is more than a right, it is a duty. Whoever triumphs in this struggle has simply accomplished his mission. Whoever fails, in spite of his honest efforts, is entitled to immortality.

ARCANE V. (E = 5.) THE MASTER OF THE ARCANES

The high priest of Isis is here represented seated between the columns of the sanctuary, one hand on a long cross with three crossbars, symbolizing the penetration of the creative genius through the three worlds. (Divine, Intellectual and Physical.) The two columns mean, respectively, the Law and the Freedom of our will-power which may obey or disobey. The other hand makes the sign of meditation and silence. At ·the feet of the high priest, two men are kneeling: a white man, personifying Good and a black man personifying Evil, both submitted to the Master of the Arcanes.

This Arcane, V., means that before you may tell a man whether he is happy or unhappy, you must find out what use he has made of his will-power, for every man is ʳeated to the image of his own works.

ARCANE VI. (U — V = 6.) THE TWO WAYS

Here the Disciple or Neophyte is seen, hesitating between two ways, each of which is pointed out to him by a woman symbolizing, the one to the right, Vice, and the one to the left, Virtue. Above, is seen a Genius holding a bow whose arrow is pointed toward Vice as a warning of the punishment that awaits the man who has preferred the easy road to vice to the hard road to virtue.

This Arcane, VI., means that one must watch over one's self, and above all show no indecision in the crucial moments of existence. Nor must one be discouraged because obstacles seem to bar the road to happiness. A strong will-power will suffice to overcome them all.

ARCANE VII. (Z = 7.) THE CHARIOT OF OSIRIS

Here we have a warrior riding a cubic chariot, upon which four columns support a starry dais; these columns symbolize the four elements, while the cubic chariot signifies that the ambition of the warrior has been realized through his will conquering every obstacle. The warrior himself has a golden band around his brow as a sign of the eternal light he is endowed with. In one hand, he holds a sword, the emblem of victory, and in his other hand, a scepter tipped with a square (Matter), a circle (Eternity), and a triangle (Divinity). He wears on his breast a Cuirass, the emblem of strength: it is adorned with three T-squares, which represent Good Judgment, Will-Power and Action. A winged sphere, on the front of the chariot, speaks of the exultation of the intellectual power in the infinite space and time. Two Sphinxes are hitched to this chariot and are now at rest. The black one represents Evil, the white one Good. They are both the slaves of the Magus when he has come out victorious from the various tests.

This Arcane, VII., means that the empire of the world belongs to those who possess

the sovereignty of the mind; that is to say the Light which reveals all the mysteries of life.

ARCANE VIII. (H = 8.) THE BALANCE AND THE SWORD

At the top of three steps which represent the three worlds, sits a woman, her brow encircled with a crown of iron, the emblem of inflexibility; her eyes are bandaged, to indicate that she holds no account of the social positions of the accused ones. A sword in one hand and a balance in the other, she judges and she punishes. The lion by her side symbolizes Force ruled over by Justice, and the Sphinx next to it, the eye of God who looks into the souls of the wicked. The winged Turtle above symbolizes Repentance which may obtain forgiveness in spite of the greatness of the crime. Finally, a divine messenger tells us that the justice of God will be the final judge of the justice of men.

This Arcane, VIII., means that everything in life is a pretty even struggle between Good and Bad, and that every action brings in its wake a re-action, thus forcing us to be most cautious in our thoughts and undertakings.

ARCANE IX. (TH = 9) THE VEILED LAMP

An old man, the symbol of wisdom, holds a lighted lamp which he covers with his mantle as a sign of discretion. He walks on, leaning on a stick, the symbol of strength acquired through experience.

This Arcane, IX., means that Wisdom has to be appealed to in every circumstance of life. It teaches one also to be discreet and silent in all critical circumstances.

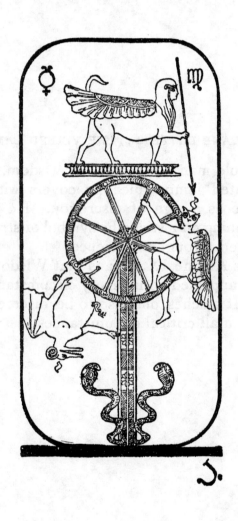

ARCANE X. (O — J — Y = 10.) THE SPHINX

We have here the most ancient drawing of the Wheel of Destiny turning upon its axis. On one side we see the God Kne-phta, the Spirit of Good; on the other side, Typhon, the Spirit of Evil, who is about to be thrown off from the wheel while the Spirit of Good is rising. Over the whole presides a full figure of a winged Sphinx representing the four forces of human nature: to Know, to Dare, to Act, to Be Silent. The Sphinx remains in perfect equilibrium as if the constantly revolving wheel of fortune had no influence over him. He thus symbolizes the mysterious power of God disposing of human destinies according to the good or bad actions of everyone. In his claws, the Sphinx holds a javelin, the emblem of supreme justice. At the foot of the supporting beam of the axis, two snakes symbolize the even forces that balance each other, while both constantly struggle for supremacy.

This Arcane, X., means that if we want only what is true, what is just, what is within our reach: if we keep silent as to our designs: if, finally, we add perseverance to the rest, we shall find ourselves one day in possession of the Key to Power.

ARCANE XI. (C — K = 20.) THE TAMED LION

We see here a young maiden opening and closing without effort the mouth of a lion, an emblem of the power over one's self acquired through the education of the will-power and the experience of life.

This Arcane, XI., means that if we are endowed with sufficient faith we may go ahead fearlessly. Obstacles are more imaginary than real. Let us find where our duty lies and accomplish it without hesitation.

ARCANE XII. (L = 30.) THE SACRIFICE

A man is hanging by one foot from a gallows stretched across the trunks of two trees the twelve branches of which have been cut off. His hands are bound and from them drop pentacles or gold pieces. One of his legs, folded down and forming with the other a reversed triangle, tells us that he dies the victim of the wicked ones. His bound hands from which drop the gold pieces, mean that ideas survive those who sacrificed themselves for them and that they will come forth later. The twelve branches that have been cut down symbolize the signs of the Zodiac who return regularly year after year.

This Arcane, XII., means that one must sacrifice one's self for others without awaiting anything but ingratitude as a reward. Forgiveness must remain our most precious gift, as it causes us to resemble more closely our Divine prototype.

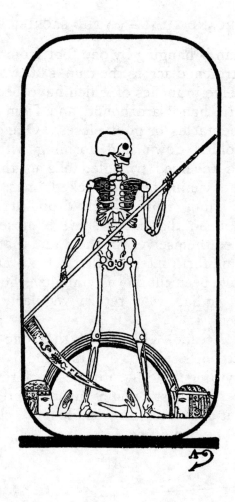

ARCANE XIII. (M = 40.) THE REAPING SKELETON

A skeleton armed with a scythe symbolizes Death mowing down human beings
whose heads, feet and hands are constantly
born again, so to speak, while a rainbow
rises in the horizon, an emblem of the immortality of the soul.

This Arcane, XIII., means that we must
raise our minds above earthly things, otherwise the bitterness of our disappointment
will shorten our days. However, if Death
should come to us early, we need not sorrow for it, since a new life and a better one
is promised us, according to our merits.

ARCANE XIV. (N = 50.) THE TWO URNS

A figure representing the Sun is transfer-
ring from a golden vase into a sliver vase
the elemental forces of nature, a symbol of
the great magic agent—the Electric and
Magnetic Fluids combined—the image of
the perpetual fecundation of Nature by
means of Light and Heat, which are also
Movement and Life.

This Arcane, XIV., means that we must
so husband our forces, moral and physical,
as to wear out all obstacles, little by little
as a drop of water pierces a stone.

ARCANE XV. (X = 60.) TYPHON

This is the Spirit of Evil, of Fatality and of Chaos. It is represented by a hippopotamus with the head of a crocodile the feet of a goat and the characteristics of man and woman. A snake emerges from his body, to show that he begets nothing but evil; his wings, like those of a bat, show him to be the Spirit of Darkness. He is seen here rising from ruins, one of his hands waving the torch of destruction and the other holding the scepter of division and hatred. At his feet are two men with goats' heads and chains around their necks, symbolizing those beings whom vice brings down lower than the beast. The horn on the figure's nose indicates his rebellion against the Divine Spirit, which he seems to be insulting.

This Arcane, XV., means that fatality will ruin your future plans if your passions are not kept in strong control by your will-power.

ARCANE XVI. (O = 70.) THE THUNDER-STRUCK TOWER

We see here a pyramid whose pinnacle is crushed down by a · stroke of lightning, throwing down two men, one of them with a crown on his head. This symbolizes the ruin of human pride and false science by the sudden influx of the Astral fluid.

This Arcane, XVI., means that you are going straight to your ruin, which will be due to your exaggerated pride, your foolish ventures and your voluntary mistakes.

ARCANE XVII. (F — P = 8o.) THE STAR OF THE MAGI

This represents a nude young girl with one foot upon the Sea and one foot upon the Earth; she represents Truth and holds two cups from which flow Kindness and Charity, the balm that alleviates human suffering. The Sea represents the bitterness of the days of sorrow. Over the young girl shines an eight-pointed star, a double symbol of the Universe and of the divine Trinity; at its center is found a white pyramid united to another pyramid, a black one and up-side-down. This is the emblem of the great occult law which is worded as follows: "That which is above is like that which is below." Seven smaller stars represent the seven Planets of Ancient Astrology. Next to the woman there is a flower with three blossoms and above the upper one a butterfly opens its wings.

This Arcane, XVII., means that if you free yourself from your lower passions and your inborn errors, and steadfastly study the mysteries of the true science you will be given the key to the mysteries of life.

ARCANE XVIII. (TS = 90.) THE TWILIGHT

Two pyramids stand on the edge of a road; in front of them two dogs howl at the moon; below, a scorpion is seen. One of the pyramids is white and is the emblem of True Science; the other pyramid is black and is the symbol of Error. The two dogs represent Good and Evil, and the scorpion is the emblem of Perversity, the worst feature of vice.

This Arcane, XVIII., means that everything is conspiring against you and you alone are kept in ignorance of the real situation. Enemies of the worst kind are plotting against you, often hiding their treachery under the garb of flattery

ARCANE XIX. (Q = 100.) THE DAZZLING LIGHT

Under a radiant sun, a young man and a
young girl hold each other by the hand
within a circle of flowers; this Arcane symbolizes love, which brings with it Happiness;
the sign within the sun above the couple is
the symbol of universal generation.

This Arcane, XIX., means that you will
be happy and no one shall take your happiness from you, if only you keep it within the
limits of the home and the sanctuary of
your heart.

ARCANE XX. (R = 200.) THE RISING OF THE DEAD

A Genius is blowing a trumpet above a Sarcophagus out of which emerge a family of father, mother and child. This not only symbolizes the Last Judgment of the Dead, but also the awakening of souls that have been put to sleep by error or inaction.

This Arcane, XX., means that you must not allow yourself to sink into sloth or forgetfulness, since you have a mission to fulfill and Providence is ready to reveal it to you as soon as you show yourself willing to accept the message.

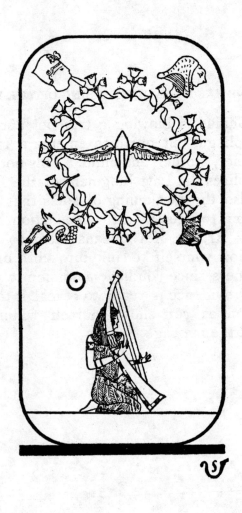

ARCANE XXI. (S = 300.) THE CROWN OF THE MAGI

We have before us a wreath made out of lotus flowers. At each of the four angles is found a head, respectively that of a lion, of a man, of an eagle and of a bull; they symbolize the four winds of the spirit, and in the center is found the primitive "lingham," the supreme Arcane of the universal generation of the three worlds, the absolute in the infinite, and the conjunction of the sexes. The wreath itself is the emblem of the magic chain that unites all beings, all things and all ideas. Under the wreath is a kneeling young girl representing Religion and playing upon a harp of three strings, the image of the triple harmony within man: Soul, Mind, Body.

This Arcane, XXI., means that you may reach the greatest height to which man may aspire; it promises you that your most ambitious desires will be realized and that your final success will only be limited by your wishes.

ARCANE XXII. (T = 4oc.) THE CROCODILE

This image, which has often been called the Atheist, or the Fool, represents a blind man with a bag on either side of his shoulder and a stick in his hand, walking towards a broken obelisk, stretched on the ground and behind which, with its huge mouth open, a crocodile awaits him. It is truly the picture of the Atheist who sees not the divine light and carries the weight of his mistakes and his faults. His stick cannot guide him, and he walks, urged on by fatality towards his ruin, symbolized by the voracious crocodile. In the sky above, the sun is partially eclipsed by a dark shadow, the symbol of Doubt destroying Faith.

This Arcane, XXII., means that a number of misfortunes are threatening you, and that your only hope is to come to you from Heaven towards which your prayers must rise constantly.

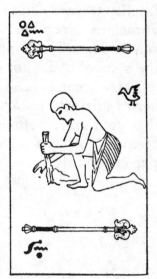

THE 56 MINOR ARCANES

ARCANE XXIII. (TH = 9.) THE MASTER OF THE SCEPTER

A King, a crown on his head, seated on his throne and pointing a scepter towards the Earth.

This Arcane, XXIII., means: Look for a powerful protector and your enterprises will succeed.

ARCANE XXIV. (E = 5.) THE MISTRESS OF THE SCEPTER

A Queen, a crown on her head, seated on her throne, with a scepter in hand.

This Arcane, XXIV., means: Your future depends on a woman; except you find her, you will not succeed.

ARCANE XXV. (U — V = 6.) THE WARRIOR OF THE SCEPTER

A man on horseback fully armed and with a scepter in his hand.

This Arcane, XXV., means that success can be obtained only by very hard work and perseverance.

ARCANE XXVI. (Z = 7.) THE SLAVE OF THE SCEPTER

A poorly-dressed man is planting a stick.

This Arcane, XXVI., means: All your labor will prove of no avail unless you abandon the foolish projects which you are entertaining now.

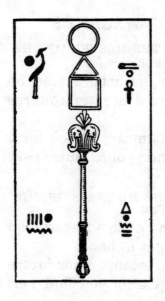

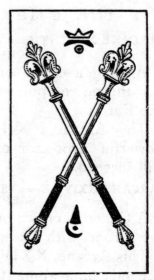

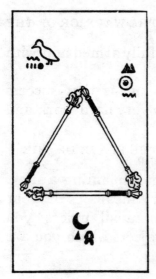

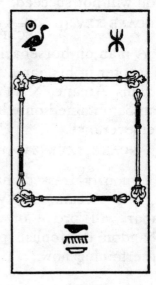

ARCANE XXVII. (A = 1.) THE SCEPTER

A Scepter tipped with a square, a triangle and a circle.

This Arcane, XXVII., means: Creative intelligence, useful labor and final success.

ARCANE XXVIII. (B = 2.) THE TWO SCEPTERS

Two Scepters arranged crosswise.

This Arcane, XXVIII., means that you will meet with great obstacles and will have to watch your interests with constant vigilance; it warns you against a partnership that will prove disastrous.

ARCANE XXIX (G = 3.) THE THREE SCEPTERS

Three Scepters arranged in a triangle.

This Arcane, XXIX., means that you will be endowed with inventive genius and will succeed in life on that account.

ARCANE XXX. (D = 4.) THE FOUR SCEPTERS

Four Scepters arranged in a square.

This Arcane, XXX., means that the enterprise you are engaged in now, will be a complete success.

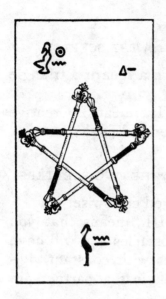

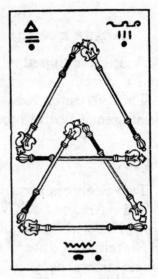

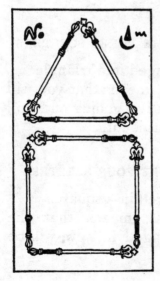

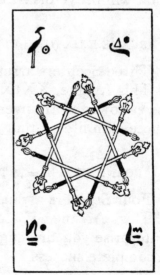

ARCANE XXXI. (E = 5.) THE FIVE SCEPTERS

Five Scepters forming a star of five rays.

This Arcane, XXXI., means that a number of favorable chances will combine to bring about the success of your enterprises, if you do not spoil everything by extravagant pride and an angry disposition.

ARCANE XXXII. (U — V = 6.) THE SIX SCEPTERS

Six Scepters arranged in two triangles.

This Arcane, XXXII., means that numerous obstacles, pitfalls and delays will surely cause the ruin of your undertakings unless your will-power shows itself strong and persevering.

ARCANE XXXIII. (Z = 7.) THE SEVEN SCEPTERS

Seven Scepters arranged in a triangle and a square, the former above the latter.

This Arcane, XXXIII., means that you have in your possession everything needed for success, especially a brilliant intelligence which will allow you to conquer all difficulties.

ARCANE XXXIV. (H = 8.) THE EIGHT SCEPTERS

Eight Scepters arranged in a star of eight rays.

This Arcane, XXXIV., means that you will meet with a great many struggles, disputes, law-suits and breaks of partnerships or marriages.

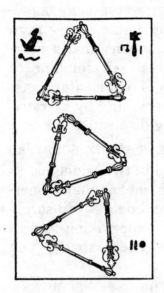

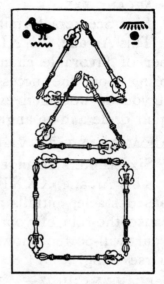

ARCANE XXXV. (TH = 9.) THE NINE SCEPTERS

Nine Scepters arranged in three triangles.

This Arcane, XXXV., means that you will be engaged in mysterious or deeply scientific enterprises whose success will depend on your prudence and discretion.

ARCANE XXXVI. (I — J — Y = 10.) THE TEN SCEPTERS

Ten Scepters, six of which are arranged in two triangles, and the four others are placed below in a square.

This Arcane, XXXVI., means that you will have to undertake a number of journeys which will prove generally successful. Wealth and fame will come to you through the arts or the sciences. There is much joy in prospect for you.

ARCANE XXXVII. (U—V=6.) THE MASTER OF THE CUP

This Arcane, XXXVII., means that you will enjoy the sincere friendship and devotion of a person in a high position. If the questioner is a woman there is a fine marriage in prospect.

ARCANE XXXVIII. (H=8.) THE MISTRESS OF THE CUP

This Arcane, XXXVIII., means, for a man, a brilliant marriage; for all questioners, the good-will of ladies of high rank.

ARCANE XXXIX. (TH=9.) THE WARRIOR OF THE CUP

This Arcane, XXXIX., means that a projected marriage will not take place and that there will be lots of troubles of all kinds on account of women.

ARCANE XL. (I—J—Y=10.) THE SLAVE OF THE CUP

This Arcane, XL., means, especially on account of the fact that the cup carried by the slave is veiled, that you will suffer from unfortunate love affairs and from the treacherous conduct of people in whom you will have unwisely placed your confidence.

ARCANE XLI. (C—K=20.) THE CUP

This Arcane, XLI., means that a passion stronger than your reason will cause your ruin.

ARCANE XLII. (L=30.) THE TWO CUPS

Two Cups within a circle.

This Arcane, XLII., means that you will enjoy a perfect union and the devotion of reciprocated love.

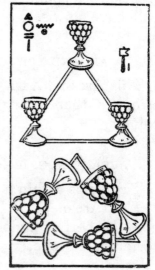

ARCANE XLIII. (M=40.) THE THREE CUPS

Three Cups arranged in a triangle; from the one at the summit emerges the head of a young girl.

This Arcane, XLIII., means the awakening of innocent affections and the early realization of your best hopes.

ARCANE XLIV. (N=50.) THE FOUR CUPS

Four Cups arranged in a square.

This Arcane, XLIV., means that a great joy is in store for you. You will meet with strong friendships and enduring love. There will soon be an increase in your family.

ARCANE XLV. (X=60.) THE FIVE CUPS

Five Cups, of which four are placed at the angles of a square, the fifth in the middle.

This Arcane, XLV., means that there will be quarrels in your marriage relations; that your love affairs will be of a dangerous nature and that your friends will prove treacherous.

ARCANE XLVI. (O=70.) THE SIX CUPS

Six Cups arranged in two triangles.

This Arcane, XLVI., means that there will be much indecision in your love affairs and that you will probably make a poor choice by not listening to the voice of your heart or to that of your conscience; there are also probabilities of divorce or of intrigues outside of wedlock.

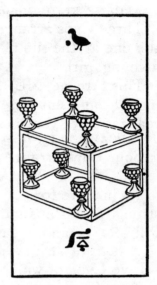

ARCANE XLVII. (F—B=80.) THE SEVEN CUPS

Seven Cups, three forming a triangle above the others arranged in a square.

This Arcane, XLVII., means the triumph of or through a woman. You will conquer your lower passions and be made happy by a congenial spouse.

ARCANE XLVIII. (TS=90.) THE EIGHT CUPS

Eight Cups arranged upon the eight angles of a cube.

This Arcane, XLVIII., means scandals due to love affairs, or unfortunate choice of husband or wife.

ARCANE XLIX. (Q=100.) THE NINE CUPS

Nine Cups, arranged in three triangles, which are all pointing downwards.

This Arcane, XLIX., means that there will be a marriage with an elderly person, but it advises you to keep away from marriage altogether.

ARCANE L. (R=20.) THE TEN CUPS

Ten Cups, nine of which are arranged in a circle with the tenth in the center.

This Arcane, L., means that you will have a happy life surrounded with affections. Your family will be numerous and your friends many. You may marry your first love.

ARCANE LI. (TS=90.) THE MASTER OF THE SWORD

This Arcane, LI., means that you will make your career in the army or some high official positions, but you will have dangerous enemies and envious rivals.

ARCANE LII. (L=30.) THE MISTRESS OF THE SWORD

This Arcane, LII., means that there are great struggles in prospect for you, due to some jealousy aroused in a woman or coming through her.

ARCANE LIII. (N=50.) THE WARRIOR OF THE SWORD

The Warrior of the Sword is riding full tilt and at great speed.

This Arcane, LIII., means that you will meet with serious dangers from fire arms or other weapons in the hands of declared enemies. You will die at an early age. A hatred will follow you relentlessly.

ARCANE LIV. (X=60.) THE SLAVE OF THE SWORD

The Slave of the Sword holds in one hand a sword and in the other a club, besides having a dagger in his belt.

This Arcane, LIV., means that you will be the object, and possibly the victim, of constant plotting. Your enemies are mean and will stop at nothing to harm you.

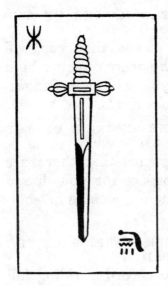

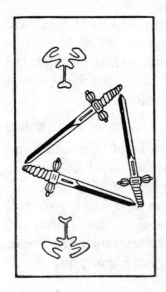

ARCANE LV. (A=1.) THE SWORD

This Arcane, LV., is a protection as well as a threat. Its meaning is modified according to the House it is found to be in. It also signifies that your enterprises will succeed in spite of great obstacles.

ARCANE LVI. (B=2.) THE TWO SWORDS

Two Swords arranged crosswise.

This Arcane, LVI., foretells a duel, but it also says that the results will not be fatal. Your partnerships will not go smoothly; and in general many obstacles will be thrown in your way.

ARCANE LVII. (G=3.) THE THREE SWORDS

Three Swords arranged in a triangle.

This Arcane, LVII., means that you have a combative disposition and are fond of strife, law-suits, etc. It is a favorable omen for all people who make a profession of fighting, but it throws shadows over all enterprises.

ARCANE LVIII. (D=4.) THE FOUR SWORDS

Four Swords arranged in a square with the points inward.

This Arcane, LVIII., announces imminent dangers; also guilty thoughts and actions, remorse and regres.

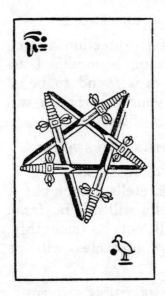

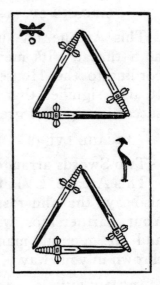

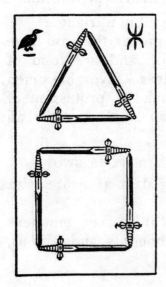

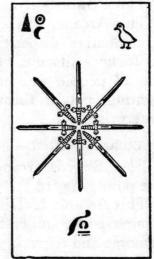

ARCANE LIX. (E=5.) THE FIVE SWORDS

Five Swords arranged in a five-pointed star.

This Arcane, LIX., means: Tendency to insanity; angers that end in murder; terrible revenge; suicide; and great danger from following first impulses blindly.

ARCANE LX. (U—V=6.) THE SIX SWORDS

Six Swords arranged in two triangles.

This Arcane, LX., means a hard struggle against adversity; also wicked temptations and great sorrows due to lack of decision.

ARCANE LXI. (Z=7.) THE SEVEN SWORDS

Seven Swords arranged, four of them in a square, and three underneath in a triangle.

This Arcane, LXI., means a sudden catastrophy that may affect the brain; a loss of position; ultimate triumph.

ARCANE LXII. (H=8.) THE EIGHT SWORDS

Eight Swords, pointing outwards and arranged in an eight-ray star.

This Arcane, LXII., means that you are threatened with the loss of a law-suit; that great anxieties are in store for you; you may even be sentenced to a heavy penalty, prison or death.

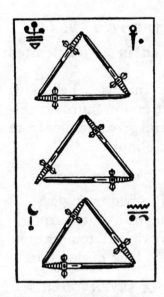
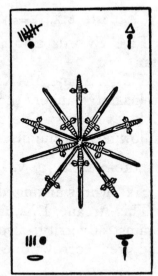

ARCANE LXIII. (TH=9.) THE NINE SWORDS

Nine Swords arranged in three triangles, points downwards.

This Arcane, LXIII., means for you sorrows, mysterious struggles, danger of death by murder, or dangerous wounds. You may triumph if you are prudent and discreet.

ARCANE LXIV. (I—J—Y=10.) THE TEN SWORDS

Ten Swords arranged in a circle with the points alternately turned in and out.

This Arcane, LXIV., means a succession of gains and losses, of quiet times and of struggles; you will be your worst enemy.

ARCANE LXV. (N=50.) THE MASTER OF THE PENTACLE *

This Arcane, LXV., means a rise in your fortune through the protection of influential people, generally of the other sex.

ARCANE LXVI. (O=70.) THE MISTRESS OF THE PENTACLE

This Arcane, LXVI., announces a brilliant marriage or, in general, the influence of one in high position willing to help you.

---

* To fully explain the next 14 Arcanes we must say that the "Pentacle" seems to mean a coin worn as a charm; in some translations it is called a "talisman" or "amulet," in others simply "money."

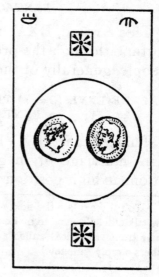

ARCANE LXVII. (TS=90.) THE WARRIOR OF THE
                        PENTACLE

This Arcane, LXVII., means that there is
lots of good luck in store for you, after
going through severe tests. There will be
many ups and downs in your life.

ARCANE LXVIII. (Q=100.) THE SLAVE OF THE
                         PENTACLE

The Slave stretches his hands towards the
Pentacle which he does not seem to be able
to grasp, because his left foot is chained to
a ball made of silver.

This Arcane, LXVIII., especially if it is
united to Jupiter, means an exaggerated love
of money and heavy losses through the un-
wise speculations of the questioner. The
result will be utter poverty.

ARCANE LXIX. (C—K=20.) THE CROWNED PEN-
                         TACLE

This Arcane, LXIX., is also called "The
Talisman of Fortune."

It means that, providing the questioner
behaves in an absolutely correct manner
and remains both wise and level-headed, he
shall reach the highest goal.

ARCANE LXX. (L=30.) THE TWO PENTACLES

Two Pentacles surrounded by a circle.

This Arcane, LXX., means that fortune
will prove fickle but that there are chances
of a profitable partnership or marriage.

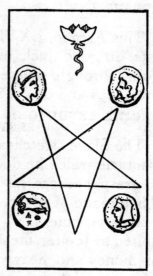

ARCANE LXXI. (M=40.) THE THREE PENTACLES

Three Pentacles arranged in a triangle.

This Arcane, LXXI., foretells that you are to secure wealth through enterprises which will be conducted by you wisely and with unremitting activity.

ARCANE LXXII. (N=50.) THE FOUR PENTACLES

Four Pentacles arranged in a square.

This Arcane, LXXII., means amassing a fortune which will be kept to the end of life.

ARCANE LXXIII. (X=60.) THE FIVE PENTACLES

Five Pentacles, four of which are arranged in a square, the fifth one in the middle.

This Arcane, LXXIII., means that you will lead a dissipated life and squander your fortune as well as lose all chances of future prosperity. If any money comes to you it will be ill-gotten gain.

ARCANE LXXIV. (O=70.) THE SIX PENTACLES

Six Pentacles arranged in two triangles.

This Arcane, LXXIV., means that you will be suddenly enriched, but this money for which you will have made no effort and given no labor will not profit you long, especially on account of the undesirable friendships which you will form. In old age, you will find yourself very poor indeed.

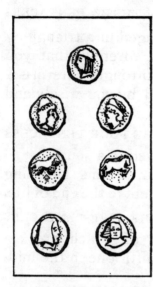

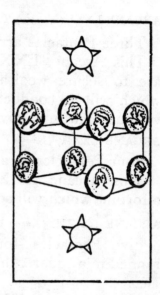

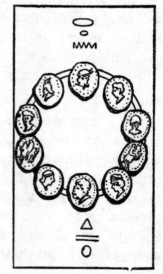

ARCANE LXXV. (F—P=80.) THE SEVEN PEN-
TACLES

Seven Pentacles, arranged three in a triangle above four in a square.

This Arcane, LXXV., means that there is
a high fortune in store for you, due to your
own personal efforts unassisted by anyone.

ARCANE LXXVI. (TS=90.) THE EIGHT PEN-
TACLES

Eight Pentacles, each one placed on one
of the eight angles of a cube.

This Arcane, LXXVI., means that you
will have to go through lengthy litigations
on account of some property, probably inherited. You may become rich in the law
profession. You may acquire money by
wrong means, but it will not profit you long.

ARCANE LXXVII. (Q=100.) THE NINE PENTACLES

Nine Pentacles arranged in three columns.

This Arcane, LXXVII., means that fortune will come to you through some mysterious means, either by discoveries or by
the death of aged relatives in far-off countries. You are recommended to be very
cautious if you want to secure that fortune.

ARCANE LXXVIII. (R=200.) THE TEN PENTACLES

Ten Pentacles arranged in a circle.

This Arcane, LXXVIII., means that you
will acquire a large fortune by your own
efforts; but you will have to defend it.